Lectures on the "Expedient Means" and "Life Span" Chapters of the Lotus Sutra

by Daisaku Ikeda

1 – the "Expedient Means" Chapter

ISBN-13: 978-1-932911-08-4
ISBN-10: 1-932911-08-1

Published by World Tribune Press
Copyright © 1995 the Soka Gakkai
All rights reserved
10 9 8

Printed in the United States of America

Daisaku Ikeda was born in Tokyo on January 2, 1928. A graduate of Fuji Junior College, he joined Soka Gakkai in 1947. He became president of Soka Gakkai International in 1975, and honorary president of Soka Gakkai in 1979.

Mr. Ikeda has also founded several institutions, including Soka University, Soka Women's Junior College, Soka Junior and Senior High Schools, Soka Elementary School, Soka Kindergarten, Min-On Concert Association, Institute of Oriental Philosophy and the Fuji Art Museum.

A poet laureate, Mr. Ikeda has received awards and honorary degrees from institutions and universities around the world, including the United Nations Peace Award. He has made numerous proposals on peace, disarmament, culture and education, and is also the author of many books ranging from Buddhist studies, novels and poetry to essays and travel diaries. His writings have been translated into more than a dozen languages.

Quotations from the Lotus Sutra have been taken from *The Lotus Sutra*, trans. Burton Watson, (New York: Columbia University Press, 1993). They are referenced in the following format: (LS2, 24), which, in this example, refers to the second chapter, p. 24.

1 — Preliminary Thoughts

Impressions of My Mentor's State of Life

TO this day, memories of my mentor, Josei Toda, the second Soka Gakkai president, lecturing on the Lotus Sutra, come vividly to mind like scenes in a great painting.

After World War II, the Soka Gakkai was in a state of ruin as a result of the campaign of suppression waged against it by the militarist government. At that time, President Toda began efforts to reconstruct the organization by delivering lectures on the Lotus Sutra to a handful of members.

I was a participant in the seventh series of lectures he gave, which began on September 13, 1948. That was in the autumn of my twenty-first year. The venue was the old Soka Gakkai Headquarters in Nishi-Kanda, Tokyo.

"I see that everyone's arrived," he began. There were fifty to sixty people present. President Toda, his eyes sparkling behind his glasses, gazed around the meeting place, which consisted of two small rooms. Then he cleared his throat and began lecturing in a frank and open manner.

I was instantly awestruck, electrified by the profound ideas, the great and intense confidence, the compassionate cry of concern for the world and humankind that seemed to gush from his very being.

President Toda would never make things deliberately difficult or complex. His lectures were intelligible, straightforward and lucid. Yet, they glowed with the light of extremely profound truth. They conveyed philosophy rooted directly in life experience and in the Law that pervades the infinite universe. They were filled with breathtaking drama and joyous music. At one point, as I listened to him speak, the sun seemed to rise in my heart, and everything became illuminated brilliantly before my eyes.

That night, still filled with the thrill and excitement I felt during the lecture, I wrote a poem in the pages of my journal:

How I marvel at the greatness and profundity of the Lotus Sutra.
Isn't it the path to salvation for all humankind?
The teaching that enlightens one to the origin of life and the universe,
The fundamental principle revealed to enable all people to acquire the loftiest character and happiness.

I am 21 years old.
Since setting out on my journey of life, what did I contemplate, what did I do, what did I make the wellspring of my happiness?
From this day on, I will advance bravely.
From this day on, I will live resolutely.
I will live within the life of the Great Law, win over my sufferings.
True sadness inspires one to lead a great life.
I now see the true Great Path and perceive the true nature of life.

Lectures on the "Expedient Means" Chapter • 7

Astonished at his profundity and breadth of knowledge, someone once asked President Toda, "When did you study these things?"

Smiling warmly, he replied: "While in prison during the persecution, I chanted sincere daimoku, and I studied. As a result, these things seem to have come back to me. The eighty thousand sutras in fact refer to my own life."

These lectures arose from the vast state of life of President Toda, who had awakened to the essence of Buddhism while in prison.

The Lotus Sutra of the Former, Middle and Latter Days

LATER on, President Toda developed the format for his lectures on the Lotus Sutra. He instituted beginners classes on the "Expedient Means" (Hoben) and "The Life Span of the Thus Come One" (Juryo) chapters specifically for those who had recently taken faith.

His lectures, so brilliant and full of conviction, planted the essence of Buddhism in the hearts of his listeners, even without their being aware of it. For these persons new to faith, many of whom thought of Buddhism only in terms of Shakyamuni, President Toda began each series of lectures by emphasizing that the Lotus Sutra is expressed differently according to the age — depending on whether it is the Former, Middle or Latter Day of the Law.

President Toda used to say:

> Everyone casually assumes that the Lotus Sutra indicates the twenty-eight–chapter text by that name. But there are in fact three kinds of Lotus Sutra.

8 • *Daisaku Ikeda*

> The first is the Lotus Sutra of Shakyamuni. This is the twenty-eight–chapter sutra of that name; this Lotus Sutra benefited people during Shakyamuni's lifetime and during the Former Day of the Law. Presently, in the Latter Day, however, even if you should carry out the practices [of the Former Day] of reading and reciting this sutra and copying it out, you will gain no benefit thereby. Our recitation of the "Expedient Means" and "Life Span" chapters during morning and evening gongyo, however, has a different significance.

> The Lotus Sutra of the Middle Day of the Law is T'ien-t'ai's *Maka Shikan* (Great Concentration and Insight). The Lotus Sutra for this period of the Latter Day is Nam-myoho-renge-kyo, the "seven-character Lotus Sutra" hidden in the depths of the "Life Span" chapter. You need to understand that there are three kinds of Lotus Sutra and how they are related to one another.

> In addition to these, there is another Lotus Sutra that, while not historically substantiated, was recognized alike by Nichiren Daishonin, Shakyamuni, T'ien-t'ai and Dengyo; this is the "twenty-four–character Lotus Sutra" expounded by Bodhisattva Never Disparaging (Fukyo).

Shakyamuni of India taught the "twenty-eight–chapter Lotus Sutra" for those alive during his lifetime and in the Former Day. T'ien-t'ai of China expounded the *Maka Shikan* for human beings of the Middle Day of the Law. And Bodhisattva Never Disparaging expounded the so-called "twenty-four–character

Lotus Sutra" for the people of the Middle Day of the Buddha called Awesome Sound King (Ionno).

President Toda explained that despite the differences in the age and the form in which the teaching was expressed, these are all in fact the same Lotus Sutra. President Toda called the Lotus Sutra as thus conceived the "manifold Lotus Sutra."

The Lotus Sutra, therefore, is not simply the "Lotus Sutra of Shakyamuni." It is also the "Lotus Sutra of T'ien-t'ai" and the "Lotus Sutra of Bodhisattva Never Disparaging." This was a stunning perspective that only President Toda, who had become enlightened to the essence of the Lotus Sutra, could have revealed.

In the course of listening to his broad-ranging lectures, his listeners, as a matter of course, could engrave distinctions between the "Lotus Sutra of Shakyamuni" and the "Lotus Sutra of Nichiren Daishonin" in their lives.

Nam-myoho-renge-kyo Is the Lotus Sutra of the Latter Day

WHAT do the different expressions of this "manifold Lotus Sutra" have in common? Ultimately, it is the teaching that "everyone equally has the potential to attain Buddhahood." There are, however, great differences in the forms whereby Shakyamuni and Nichiren Daishonin expressed this teaching.

Whereas Shakyamuni expressed it as the "twenty-eight–chapter Lotus Sutra," Nichiren Daishonin, to enable all human beings of the Latter Day to attain Buddhahood, revealed the ultimate truth of the Lotus Sutra as Nam-myoho-renge-kyo.

In the "Essence of the Lotus Sutra" (Hokke Shuyo Sho) the Daishonin says: "I, Nichiren, have abandoned the comprehensive and the abbreviated, and selected the essential. The essence is the five characters of Myoho-renge-kyo transmitted to Bodhisattva Superior Practices (Jogyo)" (GOSHO ZENSHU, P. 336).

The five characters of Myoho-renge-kyo, which constitute the Lotus Sutra's essence — that is Nam-myoho-renge-kyo of the Three Great Secret Laws — are the Lotus Sutra appropriate to this age of the Latter Day of the Law. President Toda therefore termed the Daishonin's teaching the "Lotus Sutra of the Latter Day."

The Lineage of Votaries of the Lotus Sutra

ONE who expounds a teaching that can enable all people to attain Buddhahood is certain to encounter persecution. Even Shakyamuni underwent a succession of great persecutions.

Moreover, the Lotus Sutra itself states that whoever spreads the Lotus Sutra in the Latter Day of the Law is certain to encounter numerous persecutions even greater than those Shakyamuni faced. This is clearly shown in such phrases as: "Since hatred and jealousy toward this sutra abound even when the Thus Come One is in the world, how much more will this be so after his passing?" (LS10, 164); "It [the Lotus Sutra] will face much hostility in the world and be difficult to believe" (LS14, 207); "the three powerful enemies" (LS13); and "the six difficult and nine easy acts" (LS11).

A votary who endures all of these great persecutions and perseveres in spreading the teaching among the people embodies the heart of the Lotus Sutra. Enduring persecution to spread the teaching to others is, in fact, an expression of compassion.

Just as the sutra predicts, the life of Nichiren Daishonin, who appeared in the Latter Day, was a succession of great persecutions. The Daishonin, noting that he had encountered persecutions matching in every respect those that the sutra predicts will befall its votary, declares himself to be the "votary of the Lotus Sutra in the Latter Day" and the "Buddha of the Latter Day."

At the same time, the Daishonin also designates Shakyamuni, T'ien-t'ai and Dengyo as votaries of the Lotus Sutra of their respective ages. They were all predecessors who expounded the Lotus Sutra out of their desire for the people's happiness, and who were persecuted as a result.

In addition, in many places in the Gosho, the Daishonin praises and offers the greatest encouragement to his followers by calling them "votaries of the Lotus Sutra." One such follower was Shijo Kingo, who struggled to overcome great difficulties and persevered in faith without begrudging his life. To one woman (the mother of Oto Gozen) who visited him in exile on the island of Sado, bringing her young daughter with her on the arduous journey, he goes so far as to say, "You are undoubtedly the foremost votary of the Lotus Sutra among the women of Japan" (MW-3, 52). And he gives her the name Nichimyo Shonin (Sage Nichimyo).

Buddhism Means Taking Action — Among People and in Society

THE Daishonin also writes, "At the time of kosen-rufu, all people in the entire world will become votaries of the Lotus Sutra" (GOSHO ZENSHU, P. 834). He thus indicates the principle that anyone in the world may become a votary of the Lotus Sutra.

"Votaries of the Lotus Sutra" refers to those who dedicate themselves to the mission of saving all people throughout the entire world and over the ten thousand years and more of the Latter Day of the Law. And "kosen-rufu" indicates a situation in which individuals, basing themselves on the Mystic Law, contribute to others and to society as "votaries," that is, as people of action.

Accordingly, the Soka Gakkai's first and second presidents, Tsunesaburo Makiguchi and Josei Toda, who struggled against the country's militarist regime and propagated the True Law for the people's happiness without begrudging their own lives, certainly have a place in this lineage of votaries of the Lotus Sutra.

The sixty-fifth high priest, Nichijun, lauded President Makiguchi as "an emissary of the Buddha from birth," and he praised President Toda as "the forerunner of the Bodhisattvas of the Earth."

President Toda initiated the great struggle to spread the "Lotus Sutra of the Latter Day" for those laboring in extreme distress under the conditions that ensued following World War II.

"I want to banish the word *misery* from this world." "I want to rid the world of poverty and sickness." This passionate cry of my mentor, who had stood up alone after the war, still resounds in my ears. This cry of the spirit is none other than the "heart of the Lotus Sutra."

Buddhism always means action and practice. Enabling people to overcome their difficulties and establish lives of supreme happiness requires dialogue, thoroughgoing dialogue. In such action and practice beats the "heart of the Lotus Sutra."

The 'Buddhism Hidden in the Depths of the Sutra' Is Open to All

IN the course of his lectures, President Toda often spoke as follows:

> Nichiren Daishonin read the Lotus Sutra from the standpoint of its most profound depths. The Great Teacher T'ien-t'ai read the surface or literal meaning of the Lotus Sutra and interpreted its passages and phrases most skillfully....
>
> When I say Nichiren Daishonin read the Lotus Sutra, bear in mind that he was not reading the Lotus Sutra Shakyamuni expounded just as it was, he was reading it in terms of the meaning contained in its depths, from his state of life as the Buddha of the Latter Day. This is what he indicates when he refers to "the theoretical teaching as I read it" and "the 'Life Span' chapter from the perspective of my enlightenment."

In his lectures, President Toda strictly distinguished between the literal, surface meaning, or the interpretation from the standpoint of Shakyamuni and T'ien-t'ai, and the implicit meaning, or the interpretation from the standpoint of Nichiren Daishonin, and he explained the correct way to read the sutra in the Latter Day.

Just what does it mean to read the sutra in terms of its implicit meaning in the 'Life Span' chapter? In a nutshell, it is to read the sutra from the standpoint of the vast state of life of the original Buddha, who desires to enable all people of the Latter Day to attain true happiness.

The Daishonin "read the Lotus Sutra with his life" by practicing with the spirit of not begrudging his life. The essence of the Lotus Sutra the Daishonin risked his life to propagate is Nam-myoho-renge-kyo, or the "Lotus Sutra of the Latter Day," the "Lotus Sutra hidden in the depths of the sutra."

Considered from this standpoint, the twenty-eight–chapter Lotus Sutra becomes in its entirety an explanation of Nam-myoho-renge-kyo. Reading the Lotus Sutra from the standpoint of Nam-myoho-renge-kyo, hence, is to read it from the standpoint of its implicit meaning.

When we recite the "Expedient Means" and "Life Span" chapters during gongyo, we do so not from the standpoint of the Lotus Sutra of the Former or Middle Day of the Law but from that of Nichiren Daishonin's teaching of Nam-myoho-renge-kyo.

Living Interpretation of Great Wisdom for People's Happiness, Rooted in Daily Life

NICHIREN Daishonin lectured on the twenty-eight–chapter Lotus Sutra from the standpoint of the teaching hidden in its depths, and Nikko Shonin recorded his lectures in the form of the "Ongi Kuden" (Record of the Orally Transmitted Teachings). To revive the heart of the Lotus Sutra and enable all people of the Latter Day to attain Buddhahood, the Daishonin, out of his immense compassion, explains exactly how the passages of the sutra should be read.

Reading the Lotus Sutra in terms of its implicit meaning might be described as an "interpretation from the standpoint of the Daishonin's enlightenment." It is not simply a theoretical explanation of the sutra but an interpretation that articulates the spirit of the sutra passages from the single perspective of how to enable all people, who live amid the realities of daily life, to become happy.

In other words, it is a living interpretation of the Lotus Sutra — an interpretation for putting the sutra into practice in our lives; an interpretation from the viewpoint of the human being; an interpretation for ordinary people; an interpretation that focuses on people's daily lives. It is not an interpretation merely for the sake of intellectual knowledge but an interpretation based great wisdom so as to ensure that the sutra's teaching may be developed correctly and boldly in response to the needs of the times and society.

"Hidden in the depths" may give an impression of some mystery closed off to most people. But that is certainly not the case. On the contrary, the true value of the "Buddhism hidden in the depths" lies in its being widely opened to all people and becoming a living, pulsing force that invigorates the age and society.

The members of the Nikken sect have turned this basic tenet completely on its head. They twist the teaching of the "Buddhism hidden in the depths," get hung up on merely exegetical interpretations, and cloak themselves in a shell of authority. They have turned the world of priests and temples into a world of special privilege, and they have turned the Gohonzon into a tool for controlling people. While not carrying out a satisfactory practice themselves, they spend their time in degenerate pursuits, allowing the roots of their humanity to decay. Their conduct is truly fearful. They have killed the Daishonin's spirit.

In this series, with the "Ongi Kuden" — the Daishonin's lectures on the Lotus Sutra — and the lectures of my mentor, President Toda, as my basis, I also hope to conduct my lectures in a way relevant to modern times and society.

The Benefit of Reciting the Sutra

AS you know, chanting Nam-myoho-renge-kyo, or the daimoku of the Lotus Sutra, is termed the "primary practice" and reading or reciting the "Expedient Means" and "Life Span" chapters is called the "supplementary practice" or "supporting practice."

The twenty-sixth high priest, Nichikan, explains the relationship between the primary and supplementary practices by comparing them to food and seasoning, respectively. In other words, when eating rice or noodles, the "primary" source of nourishment, you use salt or vinegar as seasoning to help bring out, or "supplement," the flavor.

The benefit from carrying out the primary practice is immense. When you also recite the "Expedient Means" and "Life Span" chapters, it has the supplementary function of increasing and accelerating the beneficial power of the primary practice. Our basic way of gongyo is to chant daimoku as its primary component and recite the "Expedient Means" and "Life Span" chapters as the supplementary.

The benefit of chanting daimoku is immeasurable and boundless. Indeed, there is infinite power in chanting Nam-myoho-renge-kyo just one time. The Daishonin says, "If you recite these words of the daimoku once, then the Buddha nature of all living beings will be summoned and gather around you" (MW-5, 112). Also, he teaches that the benefit of chanting one daimoku is equal to that of reading the entire Lotus Sutra, that of chanting ten daimoku is equal to reading the sutra ten times, that of a hundred daimoku is equal to reading the sutra a hundred times, and that of a thousand daimoku is equal to reading the sutra a thousand times.

Accordingly, we do not necessarily have to recite the sutra as we usually do in gongyo if, for example, we are sick. If, as a result of forcing ourselves to do a complete gongyo at such times, our condition should worsen, then, rather than increasing our benefit, it may in fact have the opposite effect of destroying our joy in faith and thus generating negative value.

At such times, it may be best to simply read the "Expedient Means" and verse portion (*jigage*) of the "Life Span" chapter and chant daimoku, or to just chant daimoku. Buddhism is reason.

The important thing, therefore, is for each person to make wise judgments so that he or she can carry out a practice of gongyo filled with joy at all times.

The Lotus Sutra As Read From the Daishonin's Standpoint

THE primary practice of the Daishonin's Buddhism is to chant Nam-myoho-renge-kyo, the ultimate truth of the highest Buddhist teaching. Since we are carrying out the supreme primary practice, anything less than the highest supplementary practice would be of no help at all.

The supplementary practice the Daishonin chose is the recitation of the "Expedient Means" and "Life Span" chapters of the Lotus Sutra, the purpose of Shakyamuni Buddha's advent in this world. Of the sutra's twenty-eight chapters, these two represent "the essence of the theoretical teaching" and "the essence of the essential teaching," respectively.

During the Daishonin's time, as well, his followers recited these two chapters. In one Gosho, for example, he says:

> Among the entire twenty-eight chapters, the ["Expedient Means" and "Life Span" chapters] are particularly outstanding. The remaining chapters are all in a sense the branches and leaves of these two chapters. Therefore for your regular recitation, I recommend that you practice reading the prose sections of the ["Expedient Means" and "Life Span"] chapters. (MW-6, 10)

He teaches that since the "Expedient Means" and "Life Span" chapters constitute the core of the Lotus Sutra's twenty-eight chapters, these two should be read daily.

Gongyo and daimoku are the roots that, as it were, enable you to grow into a great tree. The tree of one's life strengthens and thickens as a cumulative result of continuing the practice of gongyo and chanting daimoku. While it may not be possible to see any changes from one day to the next, because of the daily nourishment a consistent practice affords, our lives will one day become towering and vast like great trees. As we carry out a steady practice, we will develop a state of life of absolutely indestructible happiness.

As I mentioned earlier, however, it goes without saying that the "Expedient Means" and "Life Span" chapters we recite are those of the Lotus Sutra as seen from Nichiren Daishonin's standpoint of the "teaching hidden in the depths."

Nichikan explains that we read the "Expedient Means" chapter to "refute" its surface meaning and "borrow" its phrases, and that we read the "Life Span" chapter to "refute" its surface meaning and "use" the profound meaning implicit in the chapter. Reading these chapters from the standpoint of the Daishonin's Buddhism, we refute their surface meaning; it is as though we are saying: "The Lotus Sutra of Shakyamuni has no power of benefit in the Latter Day."

At the same time, from the Daishonin's standpoint, we also recite the Lotus Sutra because it "praises the greatness of the Gohonzon." This way of reading it corresponds to "borrowing" and "using" its words.

While there are meticulous arguments to support and substantiate this explanation, for the time being I will simply confirm the point that in reading the "Expedient Means" and "Life Span" chapters, we do so from the standpoint of the Daishonin's Buddhism.

Your Chanting Voices Reach the Buddhas and Bodhisattvas

SOME of you, I imagine, may wonder how reading sutra passages you cannot understand could bring about any benefit. Let me reassure you that definitely there is benefit from carrying out this practice.

The Daishonin says:

> A baby does not know the difference between water and fire, and cannot distinguish medicine from poison. But when he sucks milk, his life is nourished and sustained. Although one may not be versed [in various sutras]...if one listens to even one character or one phrase of the Lotus Sutra, one cannot fail to attain Buddhahood. (MW-7, 104–05)

Just as a baby is nourished grows naturally of it own accord by drinking milk, if you earnestly chant the Mystic Law with faith in the Gohonzon, definitely your life will come to shine with immeasurable good fortune and benefit.

To cite another example: Dogs have a language in the world of dogs, and birds have a language in the world of birds. While people cannot understand these languages, fellow dogs and fellow birds can certainly communicate within their own species.

Also, even though some people do not understand scientific jargon or a particular language, others can communicate very well through these languages.

Similarly, it might be said that when we are doing gongyo or chanting daimoku, we are speaking in the language of Buddhas and bodhisattvas. Even though you may not understand what you are saying, your voice definitely reaches the Gohonzon, all Buddhist gods and all Buddhas and bodhisattvas over the three existences and in the ten directions; and that, in response, the entire universe bathes you in the light of good fortune.

At the same time, it is certainly true that if you study the meaning of the sutra based on this practice and with a seeking mind, you can as a matter of course deepen your confidence and strengthen your faith still further.

A Practice for Revitalization

WHEN we do gongyo and chant daimoku, we conduct a ceremony in which we praise the Gohonzon and the great Law of Nam-myoho-renge-kyo. On one level, it could be said that gongyo is a paean or a song of the highest and utmost praise for the Buddha and for Nam-myoho-renge-kyo, the fundamental law of the universe. At the same time, when we do gongyo, we also praise the eternal life of the universe and the world of Buddhahood in our own lives.

President Toda once said:

> When we turn to the east and salute the Buddhist gods, then and there the Buddhist gods within our own hearts

> appear in the universe around us. Then, when we face the Gohonzon during the second prayer, the Buddhist gods all take their seats behind us.
>
> If I were to salute the Buddhist gods right now, then, regardless of whether it was night or day, they would all take their seats behind me and salute the Gohonzon. And these Buddhist gods would all start to work to fulfill my desires. This is how it works.

When we worship the Gohonzon, right then and there the doors of the microcosm within us open completely to the macrocosm, and we can experience a great and serene sense of happiness, as though gazing out over the entire universe. We savor tremendous fulfillment and joy, and gain access to a great and all-embracing wisdom. The microcosm that is encompassed by the universe in turn encompasses the entire universe.

Gongyo is an invigorating "ceremony of time without beginning" that revitalizes us from the very depths of our being. Therefore, the important thing is to do gongyo each day filled with a feeling of rhythm and cadence — like a horse galloping through the heavens. I hope you will do the kind of satisfying gongyo that leaves you refreshed and revitalized in both body and mind.

The 'King of Sutras,' Which Makes People Strong and Wise

THE Lotus Sutra is the "king of sutras," the "scripture that calls out to all people." It is a scripture "living" right now; it embodies the Buddha's compassion and egalitarian outlook. It is a "renaissance scripture," overflowing with the spirit of revitalization, which makes human beings strong and wise. And the "Expedient Means" and "Life Span" chapters are the heart of the sutra.

No practice is as universally accessible to all people as the practice of reading the sutra and chanting daimoku set forth by Nichiren Daishonin. This is the Buddhist practice that is most wide-open and accessible to all people.

During the Daishonin's lifetime, both priests and lay people assiduously recited the sutra and chanted daimoku. In modern society, however, for many people in Japan, sutras have become something distant and remote; the only exposure that most people in Japan have to the sutras is when they hear priests intoning them at funerals.

This state of affairs, this tendency to depend on priests — which has come to be regarded as so natural that no one questions it — has produced a spiritual foundation of blind obedience to religious authority. And it is the "fundamental evil" that has allowed members of the clergy to grow arrogant and decadent.

Today, however, as a result of the development of the Soka Gakkai International, people not only in Japan but throughout the world joyously chant the Mystic Law and recite the "Expedient Means" and "Life Span" chapters. This is a grand undertaking wholly without precedent in the history of Buddhism. This represents the great religious revolution of the twentieth century.

Nichiren Daishonin's "Buddhism of the people" is generating a great light of peace and happiness throughout the world. Millions are experiencing the beneficial power of the Mystic Law and acting out the wonderful drama of their human revolution. More than anything else, this fact attests most eloquently to the correctness of the SGI, which carries on the spirit of the Lotus Sutra in the present age.

As I work on these lectures, I have images of these many friends in mind. I will proceed as though carrying on a discussion with each of you while gazing up into a clear, blue sky, or strolling leisurely along a path through a field filled with fragrant, blooming flowers.

2 — Behold the Sun of Buddhahood in Your Heart

On the 'Expedient Means' Chapter

PRACTICING the Lotus Sutra causes the sun to rise in our hearts. No matter how stormy our situation, when the sun blazes in the depths of our lives, a clear, bright sky — like the blue sky of May — opens in our hearts. And when we possess in our hearts the four virtues of eternity, happiness, true self and purity, then the land — the place where we are — shines as the land of eternally tranquil light.

While everyone has a sun in his or her heart, all too few are aware it exists. The Lotus Sutra is the scripture that reveals the brilliant sun of Buddhahood inherent in our lives.

"You, yourself, are a Buddha." "Revere the sun of Buddhahood in your own life." This is the essential teaching of the Lotus Sutra, the message of the "Expedient Means" chapter.

Shakyamuni perceived that everyone possesses Buddhahood just as he did. And he made it possible for anyone to advance along the path to which he became enlightened. Based on the irrefutable reason of the proposition that all human beings are respectable, and that there is no human being who is better than anyone else, Shakyamuni went out among the people and began expounding the Law continuously.

Buddhism Is the Path of Limitless Self-improvement

IN the latter half "Expedient Means," Shakyamuni explains that the reason Buddhas appear in the world is to "open the door of," "show," "cause living beings to awaken to" and "induce them to enter the path of" the Buddha wisdom that inherently exists in human life. He further states that all people can equally develop the Buddha's state of life; and that by expounding the Lotus Sutra that enables them to do so, he has fulfilled a vow he made long ago.

I think the spirit of "Expedient Means," as expressed in these passages, is a profound form of humanistic education. The reason for this is that Buddhism starts from the recognition of each person's infinite potential. And it teaches the means whereby people can awaken to, and draw forth, the supreme treasure of Buddhahood in their lives.

When people become aware of this treasure in their own lives, they also come to recognize it in others and so will treat their fellow human beings with heartfelt respect. At the same time, they naturally take action to spark the same awareness in others.

When we make such efforts, the treasure in our own lives is polished, and this in turn enables us to develop still more confidence in our innate potential and dignity. Buddhist practice is thus the path of limitless self-improvement.

After hearing the Buddha expound "Expedient Means," Shariputra and the other voice-hearers (persons of learning) attain enlightenment. Vowing to take action among the people, they become "voice-hearers who devote themselves to the people"; they emerge as true disciples of the Buddha.

Shariputra and the others no doubt were moved by the profound compassion of their mentor, Shakyamuni. The great light of the Buddha wisdom suddenly illuminated the darkness of their formerly self-centered and tightly closed hearts. Their hearts opened and expanded widely.

They understood it had been the Buddha's intention all along to guide them to Buddhahood, the vast and boundless state of life. They realized that attaining the two vehicles (the worlds of Learning and Realization) or the three vehicles (the worlds of Learning, Realization and Bodhisattva) was not the true aim of the Buddha's teaching.

This teaching that guides people to aspire to the Buddha's state of life rather than the three vehicles is called "the replacement of the three vehicles with the one vehicle" (*kaisan ken'ichi*). The replacement of the three vehicles with the one supreme vehicle is the central teaching of the first half, or theoretical teaching, of the Lotus Sutra. And of the fourteen chapters that make up the theoretical teaching, "Expedient Means," which reveals the framework of the replacement of the three vehicles with the one supreme vehicle, is the central pillar.

In Buddhism, the term *hoben* refers to the skillful means or methods Buddhas employ to guide people to enlightenment. The "Expedient Means" (Hoben) chapter extols the wisdom of the Buddhas to thus instruct the people. Later, I will elaborate further on the profound meaning of the term *hoben*.

The Essence of the Entire 'Expedient Means' Chapter

IN our daily practice of gongyo, we recite the opening portion of "Expedient Means." This is the most important part of the entire chapter.

Briefly, the contents of this part of the chapter are as follows. First, Shakyamuni clarifies that the wisdom to which all Buddhas are enlightened is "infinitely profound and immeasurable"; and that it is well beyond the capacity of Shariputra and the other voice-hearers to comprehend. Shakyamuni then says he has employed similes and various other means to expound skillfully the Buddha wisdom to the people. Finally, he reveals that the wisdom of all Buddhas is none other than the comprehension of the "true entity of all phenomena" (*shoho jisso*). This concludes the portion of "Expedient Means" we recite each day.

In a nutshell, the "true entity of all phenomena" represents the principle that all people have the potential to be Buddhas. In other words, this passage reveals in theoretical terms the path whereby all people can attain Buddhahood. The portion we recite during gongyo is thus the very essence of the entire "Expedient Means" chapter.

Let us now proceed to the contents of "Expedient Means."

"Hoben" (Expedient Means), the second chapter of Myoho-renge-kyo

Niji seson. Ju sanmai. Anjo ni ki. Go sharihotsu. Sho-but^chi-e. Jinjin muryo. Go chi-e mon. Nange nannyu. Issai sho-mon. Hyaku-shi-butsu. Sho fu no chi.

At that time the World-Honored One calmly arose from his samadhi and addressed Shariputra, saying: "The wisdom of the Buddhas is infinitely profound and immeasurable. The door to this wisdom is difficult to understand and difficult to enter. Not one of the voice-hearers or pratyekabuddhas is able to comprehend it. (LS2, 23)

Shakyamuni at last begins to expound the teaching of the Lotus Sutra. At the beginning of "Expedient Means," Shakyamuni, having arisen from samadhi, or deep meditation, on the truth that immeasurable meanings come from the one Law, tells Shariputra straightaway: "The wisdom of the Buddhas is infinitely profound and immeasurable.... [None of you] is able to comprehend it." The teaching thus opens with a scene of considerable tension.

Regarding "At that time...," which opens the chapter, let us first consider just what kind of "time" is being indicated? President Toda explained:

> "At that time..." refers to the concept of time as employed in Buddhism. This is different from time in the sense that we ordinarily use it to indicate some particular time such as two o'clock or three o'clock, or in the sense of "springtime."
>
> Neither is "At that time..." comparable to the typical nursery tale opening, "Once upon a time...." Time, in the sense signified here, refers to when a Buddha, perceiving the people's longing for him, appears in order to expound his teaching.

Four conditions must be met for a Buddha to expound the Law — those of time, response, capacity and Law. Time, in terms of Buddhism, indicates when the Buddha appears in order to expound the Law in response to the capacity of people who seek his teaching. In other words, it refers to when a Buddha and human beings encounter one another.

Shakyamuni's Disciples Were Awaiting a Great Teaching

WHILE Shakyamuni is engaged in meditation in the "Introduction" chapter of the Lotus Sutra, the seeking spirit for the Way of his disciples, including Shariputra and others of the two vehicles, no doubt reaches a climax.

They probably thought to themselves: "I wonder what kind of teaching the World Honored One will expound?" "I don't want to miss a single word." "I will engrave his teaching in my

Lectures on the "Expedient Means" Chapter • 31

heart." While containing their blazing enthusiasm, they all strained their ears to listen. And, focusing every nerve in their bodies, they fixed their gaze on their mentor.

And so the time became ripe. Shakyamuni finally broke his long silence and began to expound the Lotus Sutra — the ultimate teaching that enables all living beings to attain Buddhahood. This is the meaning of "At that time...," which begins the "Expedient Means" chapter.

In other words, it indicates the time when a Buddha stands up to guide the people to enlightenment, and the time when the disciples have established a single-minded seeking spirit for the Buddha's teaching. It signifies a profound concordance of the hearts of the disciples with the heart of the mentor. This scene in the Lotus Sutra represents the opening of the grand drama of mentor and disciple who dedicate themselves to the happiness of humankind.

The Buddha is the one who most keenly "comprehends the time." The Buddha awaits the proper time, discerns the nature of the time, creates the time and expounds the Law that accords with the time. Such is the Buddha's wisdom and compassion.

"Why do the people suffer?" "For what do the people yearn?" "What teaching enables the people to become happy? And when should it be taught?" The Buddha ponders these matters constantly and expounds the Law freely in accordance with the time.

In this sense, to "know the time" is also to understand the hearts of the people. The Buddha is a leader who is a master at understanding the others' hearts. The Buddha is an "instructor of the spirit" and an expert on human nature.

From the Buddha's standpoint, "that time" is the time when the Buddha initiates the struggle to enable all people to attain enlightenment. And for the disciples, it is the time when they directly grasp and become powerfully aware of the Buddha's spirit.

Regarding the importance of the time, Nichiren Daishonin says, "One who wishes to study the teachings of Buddhism must first learn to understand the time" (MW-3, 79). Thus he indicates that Buddhism is expounded based on the time, and that the teaching that should be propagated is the one that accords with the time.

Proclaiming this period of the Latter Day of the Law to be the time when the Great Pure Law of Nam-myoho-renge-kyo should be spread, the Daishonin launched the struggle to propagate the Mystic Law and enable all people of the Latter Day to attain enlightenment.

One's Inner Determination to Fight Now Opens the Way Forward

IN other words, from the standpoint of the "Buddhism hidden in the depths," we can interpret "that time" as indicating the time when the original Buddha, Nichiren Daishonin, commenced his great struggle to save all humankind. And it can also be said that "that time" indicates the time when the Daishonin's disciples stand up in concert with the mentor to realize kosen-rufu.

In terms of our practice, therefore, I would like to stress that "that time" exists only when we pray to the Gohonzon and manifest determination and awareness of our mission for kosen-rufu.

We have to make a determination, pray and take action. Unless we do so, our environment will not change in the least; though five or ten years may pass, "that time" will never arrive.

Our single-minded determination for kosen-rufu, and that alone, creates the "time." "That time" is when we set our lives in motion, when we stand up of our own volition and by our own will and strength. "That time" is when we summon forth strong faith and take our place on the grand stage of kosen-rufu.

Goethe writes, "The moment alone is decisive; Fixes the life of man, and his future destiny settles." "That time" is the moment you resolve from the depths of your heart: "Now I will stand up and fight!" From that instant your destiny changes. Your life develops. History begins.

This is the spirit of the mystic principle of the True Cause (*honnin-myo*). This is the principle of *ichinen sanzen*. The moment you autonomously determine to accomplish something — not when you do it because you are told to — is "that time," the "time" of mission.

3 – Immeasurable Meanings Derive From the One Law

Niji seson. Ju sanmai. Anjo ni ki. Go sharihotsu. Sho-but^chi-e. Jinjin muryo. Go chi-e mon. Nange nannyu. Issai sho-mon. Hyaku-shi-butsu. Sho fu no chi.

At that time the World-Honored One calmly arose from his samadhi and addressed Shariputra, saying: "The wisdom of the Buddhas is infinitely profound and immeasurable. The door to this wisdom is difficult to understand and difficult to enter. Not one of the voice-hearers or pratyekabuddhas is able to comprehend it. (LS2, 23)

AT the outset of "Expedient Means," Shakyamuni arises serenely from *samadhi* and begins expounding the teaching of the Lotus Sutra. *Samadhi*, or meditative concentration, means to focus one's mind on one point so that it becomes perfectly tranquil and still like a clear mirror, and thereby enter a state of inner serenity. Shakyamuni enters samadhi early in the "Introduction," the first chapter of the sutra, and continues meditating throughout the chapter.

Even though the sutra speaks of Shakyamuni entering *samadhi*, or meditative concentration, this does not mean that in the Latter Day of the Law people should seclude themselves in mountains and forests and practice sitting meditation or contemplation. Nichiren Daishonin, who struggled in the very midst of society to enable all people to attain supreme enlightenment, rejects such practices as not suited to the time.

Needless to say, in the present age *samadhi* or "meditative concentration" means doing gongyo and chanting daimoku. We do not, however, carry out this practice of "meditative concentration" secluded in mountains and forests. Rather, on the foundation of our practice of gongyo and daimoku, each day we polish our lives, draw forth infinite wisdom and courage, and go out into society. This is the discipline we are carrying out.

Contemplation or meditation for its own sake is absurd. In the Vimalakirti Sutra, Shakyamuni clearly explains that true meditation is not solitary contemplation beneath a tree but playing an active role in society while embracing the truth.

Mahatma Gandhi, to someone who urged that he pursue a life of meditation, is said to have remarked that he felt no need to withdraw to a cave for that purpose. He carried the cave with him, he said, wherever he went. This episode is characteristic of Gandhi, who devoted his life to taking action and practicing among the people.

Buddhism is not a religion that closes its eyes to people's suffering; it is a teaching that opens people's eyes. Therefore, Buddhism is the path that enables people to become happy. To turn away our eyes from the contradictions of society and rid ourselves of all worldly thoughts is not the way of Buddhist practice.

The true spirit of meditation lies in manifesting our innate wisdom in society and resolutely struggling for the happiness of ourselves and others, and to construct a better society.

The Daishonin Stood Up for All Humankind

THE specific type of samadhi Shakyamuni entered is termed "meditation on the truth that immeasurable meanings derive from the one Law." This Law from which immeasurable meanings derive is the foundation of all teachings. Thus the Muryogi Sutra reads, "Immeasurable meanings are born from a single Law." Shakyamuni expounded the Lotus Sutra from the standpoint of this great truth to which he had become enlightened.

Nichiren Daishonin clarified that this "single Law" is Nam-myoho-renge-kyo. He revealed this fundamental Law of the universe for all people and expressed it so that anyone can practice it. He expounded it for the sake of the entire world and for all humanity.

Nichiren Daishonin stood up to expound the Law of Nam-myoho-renge-kyo for the happiness of all people. This is what the phrase "calmly arose from his samadhi" signifies in terms of its implicit meaning.

In practical terms from our own standpoint, "immeasurable meanings are born from a single Law" means precisely that by believing in and embracing the Mystic Law, we can acquire the Buddha's infinite wisdom. By doing gongyo and chanting daimoku, we cause our lives to shine with supreme wisdom and advance along the path of genuine victory in life. Each day, starting from the prime point of life, we can refresh our vitality.

Therefore, please be confident that SGI members who pray with the determination, "I will fight again today," "I will do my best tomorrow, too," and who stand up for kosen-rufu in society are themselves practicing "calmly arising from samadhi" each morning and evening.

The 'Unsolicited and Spontaneous Teaching'

SHAKYAMUNI, having arisen from *samadhi*, spontaneously begins to expound the Lotus Sutra without anyone first requesting him to do so. This manner of preaching, where the Buddha expounds the Law on his own initiative without any question having been put to him, is termed the "unsolicited and spontaneous teaching."

The doctrine Shakyamuni spontaneously and serenely begins to expound is so profound that his disciples could not have imagined it, let alone have asked him to teach it. In this, we see the outpouring of wisdom and compassion that impelled Shakyamuni to expound the Lotus Sutra.

It is of profound significance that Shakyamuni employs the "unsolicited and spontaneous teaching" format as he begins to expound the Lotus Sutra. All sutras other than the Lotus are provisional teachings expounded "according to others' minds" (*zuitai*), that is, according to the capacity of his listeners; and as such do not represent the Buddha's true intention. By contrast, the Lotus Sutra is described as "according with [the Buddha's] own mind" (*zuijii*), because in this sutra Shakyamuni reveals the truth directly, in accordance with his own enlightenment.

The Daishonin's declaration of the establishment of the Buddhism of the Latter Day of the Law is another instance of "unsolicited and spontaneous teaching." With regard to establishing his teaching, the Daishonin says: "If I speak out, I am fully aware that I will have to contend with the three obstacles and the four devils" (MW-2 [2ND ED.], 95). He knew, in other words, that if he spread the Mystic Law, he was certain to encounter persecution.

Nonetheless, without being asked by anyone, he began to expound the teaching of Nam-myoho-renge-kyo. In his lifetime struggles, the Daishonin was carrying out the practice of *zuijii*.

In terms of our own practice, *zuijii* indicates the spontaneous spirit to praise the Mystic Law out of profound recognition of its greatness, no matter what anyone might say. Such admiration for the Mystic Law is the essential reason we recite the sutra during gongyo.

Zuijii also indicates the attitude of "propagating the Law to the full extent of one's ability," the irrepressible desire to teach and explain to others even a single word or phrase. By contrast, if you talk about the Mystic Law because you have been told to do so, or in the belief that it will make others think highly of you, then you are following the practice of *zuitai*, or acting "according to others' minds."

Broadly speaking, the "unsolicited and spontaneous teaching" and the practice of *zuijii* indicate autonomous and self-motivated action. It does not matter if your words are plain, or if you are not a talented speaker; what is important is to pray earnestly with the determination for others to become happy and to tell others candidly about the greatness of Buddhism — with conviction and in your own words. This is the spirit of the Lotus Sutra, and the spirit of the Soka Gakkai.

The Buddha Seeks To Enable All People To Attain the Same Enlightened State of Life

SHAKYAMUNI starts out by telling Shariputra: "The wisdom of the Buddhas is infinitely profound and immeasurable. The door to this wisdom is difficult to understand and difficult to enter. Not one of the voice-hearers or pratyekabuddhas is able to comprehend it." This statement extols the great wisdom of the Buddha.

The "wisdom of the Buddhas" is the wisdom that shines like a sun within the Buddha. Shakyamuni praises this wisdom as being "infinitely profound and immeasurable." He calls the Buddha's wisdom "infinitely profound" because it penetrates down to the truth that is the very foundation of life. The Buddha's wisdom is said to be "immeasurable" because its light broadly illuminates all things.

The wisdom of the Buddhas profoundly and broadly illuminates and reveals life in its entirety. Therefore, the Buddha's state of life is said to be "expansive and profound." Likening the Buddha's state of life to a great tree or a mighty river, T'ien-t'ai says: "The deeper the roots, the more prolific the branches. The farther the source, the longer the stream" (MW-4, 272).

Shakyamuni is not praising the wisdom of the Buddhas to say that the Buddha alone is great. In fact, it is just the opposite; his purpose is to encourage others. In effect, he is saying: "Therefore, all of you, too, should make this same great wisdom of the Buddha shine in your own lives and become happy."

Wisdom is the path to happiness. Money, skill at "getting by" in the world, status — none of these can enable us to overcome the fundamental sufferings of birth, old age, sickness and death. The only way is to cultivate the wisdom with which our lives are inherently endowed.

The purpose of the Lotus Sutra is to enable all people to cultivate supreme wisdom in their hearts and advance along the great path of indestructible happiness. The Daishonin says, "The treasures of the heart are the most valuable of all" (MW-2 [2ND ED.], 238). That is why Shakyamuni starts out by extolling the wisdom of the Buddhas, which is the supreme wisdom.

The next passage reads, "The door to this wisdom is difficult to understand and difficult to enter." Here Shakyamuni again praises the Buddha wisdom but from a slightly different perspective.

The "door to this wisdom" is the door to the realm of Buddha wisdom. The various teachings Shakyamuni expounded were means for enabling people to enter the realm of this wisdom. Prior to the Lotus Sutra, he had expounded various teachings in accordance with his listeners' diverse capacities. At different times, for example, he taught that life is suffering; that nothing is constant; that happiness lies in extinguishing all desires; and that people should seek to awaken to the principle of dependent origination.

In this way, Shakyamuni, exercising the wisdom of the Buddha, expounded teachings that matched the various capacities of the people. However, these individual teachings did not represent the Buddha's true purpose. The purpose of his teaching, rather, lay in enabling all people to enter the path of wisdom, the path for becoming a Buddha.

This purpose of the Buddha cannot be understood by the wisdom of people of the two vehicles of Learning (voice-hearers) and Realization (*pratyekabuddhas*). Even though such people may understand the contents of his teaching, they cannot fathom his reason for expounding it.

Their very satisfaction with individual teachings that explained life's impermanence or the need to eradicate desires prevented them from entering the realm of the wisdom of the Buddha who had expounded these doctrines. They reached the gate, as it were, and then stopped. Therefore, Shakyamuni says this wisdom is "difficult to understand and difficult to enter."

Regard Suffering and Joy As Facts of Life

IN the foregoing, I have discussed the literal or surface meaning of this passage. President Toda explained this passage from the standpoint of its implicit meaning as follows:

> The line, "The wisdom of the Buddhas is infinitely profound and immeasurable" means that the wisdom of

> Nam-myoho-renge-kyo is infinitely profound and immeasurable. The passage, "The door to this wisdom is difficult to understand and difficult to enter," refers to the "door of faith" in the Gohonzon. By substituting faith for wisdom, we can enter the "door to this wisdom." This door is "difficult to understand and difficult to enter."

As the Daishonin indicates where he says, "'Wisdom' means Nam-myoho-renge-kyo" (GOSHO ZENSHU, P. 725), Nam-myoho-renge-kyo contains the infinitely profound and immeasurable wisdom of the Buddhas in its entirety. And the door to enter the wisdom of Nam-myoho-renge-kyo is the "door of faith." Thus the Daishonin says, "'Door' means faith" (Ibid., P. 715).

If we believe in the Gohonzon and exert ourselves in practice and study as the Daishonin teaches, then, in accordance with the principle of "substituting faith for wisdom," we can develop a state of life of supreme happiness. This is what it means to enter the "door of faith," to advance along the path of attaining Buddhahood in this lifetime.

However, carrying through with faith becomes difficult when we encounter waves of adversity in life. At such times, people may forget that faith is the "door of wisdom." Instead, filled with complaint, they are tossed about helplessly on the rough seas. Or again, they may fear suffering and give themselves over to lives of pleasure and ease. In this sense, as well, the "door of faith" is difficult to understand and difficult to enter.

For precisely this reason, the Daishonin says, "Regard both suffering and joy as facts of life and continue chanting Nam-myoho-renge-kyo" (MW-1, 161).

Nam-myoho-renge-kyo is the wellspring of the wisdom of all Buddhas. And gongyo is a "ceremony of *kuon ganjo*" in which we return to the very foundation of our lives and draw wisdom from the great ocean of the world of Buddhahood.

4 — The Transformation of the Voice-Hearers

Niji seson. Ju sanmai. Anjo ni ki. Go sharihotsu. Shobut^chi-e. Jinjin muryo. Go chi-e mon. Nange nannyu. Issai sho-mon. Hyaku-shi-butsu. Sho fu no chi.

At that time the World-Honored One calmly arose from his samadhi and addressed Shariputra, saying: "The wisdom of the Buddhas is infinitely profound and immeasurable. The door to this wisdom is difficult to understand and difficult to enter. Not one of the voice-hearers or pratyekabuddhas is able to comprehend it. (LS2, 23)

The Buddha's Wisdom Far Surpasses the Wisdom of People of the Two Vehicles

IN the final sentence of this passage, Shakyamuni announces to Shariputra that the vast wisdom of the Buddhas cannot be fathomed by the shallow wisdom of voice-hearers and *pratyekabuddhas*—the people of the two vehicles.

Shariputra, a voice-hearer, is known as the foremost in wisdom among Shakyamuni's disciples. In terms of wisdom, he is a brilliant intellectual, second to none. Still, Shakyamuni declares that not even Shariputra, with all his wisdom, can comprehend the wisdom of the Buddhas. As Shakyamuni continues his preaching in this and subsequent chapters, however, not only Shariputra but all the voice-hearers undergo a complete transformation. They begin to comprehend the wisdom of the Buddhas; and Shakyamuni acknowledges they can attain Buddhahood without fail. This is known as the "enlightenment of the two vehicles."

The Great Ocean of Buddhahood Can Only Be Entered Through Faith

WHAT brought about this change for the voice-hearers? What happened to them as a result of hearing Shakyamuni expound the Lotus Sutra? This is clarified in "Simile and Parable," the third chapter, where Shakyamuni explains that even Shariputra had been "able to gain entrance through faith alone." In other words, the voice-hearers can enter the supreme wisdom of the Buddhas, not through their own shallow wisdom but through faith.

In Buddhism, faith means a pure heart, a flexible spirit and an open mind. Faith is the function of human life to dispel the dark clouds of doubt, anxiety and regret, and sincerely open and direct one's heart toward something great.

Faith might also be characterized as the power that enables the microcosm of the self to sense the universal macrocosm. Through this power, the power of faith, the voice-hearers can enter the vast realm of Buddha wisdom. According to Nagarjuna and T'ien-t'ai, Buddhism is a vast ocean, and only those with faith can enter.

It would seem that Shakyamuni's preaching of the first half—or theoretical teaching—of the Lotus Sutra, which was specifically addressed to the voice-hearers, aroused in them a power of faith markedly more profound than they had previously manifested. In "Expedient Means," Shakyamuni vigorously exhorts Shariputra to further develop his faith. He is saying, in effect, "This is the time when you should summon up great power of faith."

Voice-hearers Who Simply Hear the Teaching Become Voice-hearers Who Relate It to Others

WHAT becomes of the voice-hearers who enter the realm of the wisdom of the Buddhas through faith? The voice-hearers themselves clarify this point when they say, "Now we have become voice-hearers in truth, for we will take the voice of the Buddha way and cause it to be heard by all."

In other words, they change from being "voice-hearers who hear the teaching" to being "voice-hearers who cause others to hear the teaching." They become voice-hearers who talk about Buddhism among the people.

In one sense, "voice-hearers" indicates those who look to their teacher, the Buddha, for personal salvation and gain. From this standpoint, the statement suggests that they have changed from "disciples who are saved" to "disciples who save others," "disciples who join the mentor in his struggle."

In the pre-Lotus Sutra teachings, "people of the two vehicles" means those who become attached to a partial enlightenment and lose their aspiration for the Buddha way. In the Lotus Sutra, they are revived; instead of being people of the two vehicles who close themselves off in a shallow enlightenment, they become true people of the two vehicles who seek the supreme enlightenment of the Buddha.

In essence, what is revived in the voice-hearers is trust in human beings, respect for the people and hope for the future. In other words, they discover the Buddha nature shining within all people. Such is the power and benefit of the vast Buddha wisdom they attain through faith.

A Person of Wisdom Has an Excellent Heart

WISDOM, in the Lotus Sutra, does not simply mean being smart; it is far more profound. Essentially, it is to have an excellent "heart." Wisdom signifies humanity and force of character borne of strength, breadth and profundity of spirit.

The Daishonin says, "The wise may be called human" (MW-2 [2ND ED.], 240). He also explains that one who perseveres in following a correct way of life based on the Mystic Law, unswayed by praise and censure, is truly wise (*GOSHO ZENSHU*, P. 1151).

A Canadian poet writes in effect that no one is as condescending toward others as an ignorant person; whereas a wise person has the capacity for tolerance.

Interpreting the transformation of the voice-hearers from the standpoint of the Daishonin's Buddhism, Shariputra, who enters the realm of the wisdom of the Buddhas through faith and becomes a disciple of action, represents the followers of Nichiren Daishonin who believe in and embrace Nam-myoho-renge-kyo, the entity of the wisdom of the Buddhas, and who strive to realize kosen-rufu.

Thus the Daishonin says, "Now Nichiren and his followers who chant Nam-myoho-renge-kyo are all Shariputras" (GOSHO ZENSHU, P. 722). All who conduct Buddhist dialogue with friends, and who earnestly chant the Mystic Law and tax their wisdom to help others become happy are "Shariputras" of the present age.

Daimoku Contains the Benefit of All Practices

IN this passage, Shakyamuni explains why the wisdom of the Buddhas is infinitely profound and immeasurable, and why the door to this wisdom is difficult to understand and difficult to enter, by indicating the practices he has carried out in previous lifetimes.

To convey a sense of just how difficult is the path to attaining Buddhahood, Shakyamuni explains that a Buddha has served countless Buddhas in previous lifetimes, has bravely and vigorously carried out incalculable practices, and as a result has become enlightened to a law of unparalleled greatness.

By comparison, the practice of Shariputra and the other people of the two vehicles is quite shallow. Accordingly, they cannot comprehend the true purpose of the teaching he is expounding from the standpoint of the immeasurable wisdom of the Buddhas.

Comprehension, Courage and Action Are Born of Heartfelt Agreement

IT is interesting how Shakyamuni mentions his practices in previous lifetimes to indicate that the wisdom of the Buddhas is infinitely profound and immeasurable. Since the wisdom he attained cannot itself be easily articulated, he explains it by describing the practices that became the cause for his enlightenment.

This method of reasoning may seem somewhat obscure to us today. But for the people of India at the time, the idea that one repeatedly undergoes the cycle of birth and death was a matter of common sense. Therefore, by explaining that he had served countless Buddhas in the past, Shakyamuni could readily win their understanding and agreement.

Heartfelt agreement is important. When people are satisfied with an explanation, their comprehension deepens, their state of life expands. Heartfelt agreement produces courage and hope, and is sure to give rise to action.

For this reason, dialogue is very important. The power to impart profound understanding and win others' agreement is the power of words and the power of the voice. As a result of Shakyamuni's power of speech, even Shariputra developed a seeking spirit to attain the vast wisdom of the Buddhas.

The Mystic Law Contains the Practices of All Buddhas

Sho-i sha ga. Butsu zo shingon. Hyaku sen man noku. Mushu sho butsu. Jin gyo sho-butsu. Muryo doho. Yumyo shojin. Myosho fu mon. Joju jinjin. Mi-zo-u ho. Zui gi sho setsu. Ishu nange.

"What is the reason for this? A Buddha has personally attended a hundred, a thousand, ten thousand, a million, a countless number of Buddhas and has fully carried out an immeasurable number of religious practices. He has exerted himself bravely and vigorously, and his name is universally known. He has realized the Law that is profound and never known before, and preaches it in accordance with what is appropriate, yet his intention is difficult to understand. (LS2, 23-24)

IN this section, Shakyamuni clarifies that through having carried out an immeasurable number of practices under a countless number of Buddhas, he has attained the wisdom and enlightened state of life of the Buddha.

A Buddha is one who has experienced and carried out all manner of practices in previous lifetimes. In this sense, "a Buddha" means an expert at Buddhist practice. Shakyamuni possessed in his life the experience and benefit of all the practices he

Lectures on the "Expedient Means" Chapter • 51

carried out in the past. For this reason, he could expound teachings that perfectly matched the capacity of the people and the time. A Buddha is one whose richness of experience in the past produces a spiritual abundance in the present.

True leaders are those who can offer appropriate advice based on their own rich experience, not people who just give orders and are all words and no substance. Leaders are first and foremost people of action who lead by personal example. They are not people who merely occupy some status or position. Leaders are people of hard work, not people of tactics and maneuvering; and, above all, they are not authoritarians.

In any event, the life of a Buddha is profound and wondrous. The Buddha's one life contains the benefit of immeasurable practices; all is contained in the one. Such is the mystery of life. Nichiren Daishonin expressed the mystic nature of life as Nam-myoho-renge-kyo. Thus, he writes:

> The five characters of Myoho-renge-kyo, the heart of the essential teaching of the Lotus Sutra, contain all the benefits amassed by the beneficial practices and meritorious deeds of all the Buddhas throughout the past, present and future. (MW-4, 129)

In other words, Myoho-renge-kyo contains the benefits of all practices and meritorious deeds not only of Shakyamuni but of all Buddhas throughout time and space. Daimoku contains the benefit of all practices and all meritorious deeds carried out by all Buddhas in the ten directions and over the three existences of past, present and future.

52 • *Daisaku Ikeda*

From the viewpoint of the Daishonin's Buddhism, therefore, the passage, "A Buddha has personally attended a hundred, a thousand, ten thousand, a million, countless number of Buddhas and has fully carried out an immeasurable number of religious practices," is extolling the benefit of Nam-myoho-renge-kyo.

'Earnest Faith' Is the Path To Attaining Buddhahood

IN describing the immeasurable practices he has carried out, Shakyamuni's purpose is not to indicate that others should do the same. Rather, he is saying in effect, "Based on your trust in this Buddha, you should put your faith in the teaching that I, Shakymuni, am about to expound."

Shakyamuni is a Buddha who in the past carried out immeasurable practices. The well-known tales of Sessen Doji and King Shibi describe the brave and vigorous practices he carried out in previous lifetimes.

In the Latter Day of the Law, there is no need to carry out "an immeasurable number of religious practices." Embracing and upholding the law of Nam-myoho-renge-kyo for oneself and for others, which contains "all the benefits amassed by the [Buddha's] beneficial practices and meritorious deeds," provides the benefit of carrying out "an immeasurable number of religious practices."

This is not to say, however, that Shakyamuni's practices are irrelevant to us. Throughout the Gosho, Nichiren Daishonin stresses the spirit of Shakyamuni's practice. For example, as for the meaning of Sessen Doji's practice for the people of the Latter Day, he says:

> Even common mortals can attain Buddhahood if they cherish one thing: earnest faith. In the deepest sense, earnest faith is the will to understand and live up to the spirit, not the words, of the sutras. (MW-1, 268)

In the Latter Day of the Law, earnest faith, the will to understand and live up to the Law, is the cause for attaining Buddhahood.

The Daishonin praises most highly those courageous individuals who maintain earnest faith. For example, to Shijo Kingo, who made the long and difficult journey over mountains and rivers and across the treacherous sea to visit the Daishonin in exile on Sado Island, he says, "How could your resolve be inferior to that [of Sessen Doji]?" (MW-6, 308). And to Myoichi-ama, he writes regarding her deceased husband who had dedicated his life to the Mystic Law, "How could his benefit differ from that of Sessen Doji?" (MW-1, 151).

In light of the foregoing, we can say that the earnest faith of each person who lives based on the Mystic Law and struggles for kosen-rufu contains the benefit of all practices and all meritorious deeds.

5 — A Revolutionary View of Buddhahood: 'Embracing the Gohonzon Is in Itself Enlightenment'

Sho-i sha ga. Butsu zo shingon. Hyaku sen man noku. Mushu sho butsu. Jin gyo sho-butsu. Muryo doho.

"What is the reason for this? A Buddha has personally attended a hundred, a thousand, ten thousand, a million, a countless number of Buddhas and has fully carried out an immeasurable number of religious practices. (LS2, 23)

The Teaching for Attaining Buddhahood in This Lifetime

ACCORDING to this description, a Buddha has served and practiced under an incalculable number of Buddhas for an unimaginably long time. This practice, continued over many lifetimes, becomes the cause for enlightenment; as a result, the practitioner attains the supreme state of Buddhahood. This is termed "practicing toward enlightenment over a period of countless kalpas."

We should bear in mind, however, that this is only a literal interpretation of the causes (practices) made and effects (virtues) realized by the Buddha as described in the theoretical teaching of the Lotus Sutra.

Reading this passage from the standpoint of Nichiren Daishonin's Buddhism, President Toda explained that it is not necessary for us to engage in this type of practice for countless kalpas to attain enlightenment. He discussed the meaning of this passage as follows:

> From the standpoint of the Daishonin's teaching, the Buddha [the Gohonzon] of Nam-myoho-renge-kyo is the fundamental Law that gives birth to a hundred, a thousand, ten thousand or a million Buddhas. Therefore, without undertaking any difficult or painful practices, by simply chanting Nam-myoho-renge-kyo, we gain more benefit than we could by personally attending that many Buddhas. The benefit of this single practice is equal to that of the immeasurable number of austerities carried out by all Buddhas.

Nam-myoho-renge-kyo is the fundamental Law that generates all Buddhas. To put it another way, the fundamental Law that enables all Buddhas to attain enlightenment is not that they have carried out various austerities over countless kalpas, but that they have awakened to the fundamental Law of Nam-myoho-renge-kyo. The Buddhist practice of the Latter Day of the Law is to embrace and uphold the Law of Nam-myoho-renge-kyo directly. In the Daishonin's Buddhism, therefore, it is not necessary to engage in austerities for countless kalpas to attain Buddhahood.

Nichiren Daishonin states in "The True Object of Worship": "Shakyamuni's practices and the virtues he consequently attained are all contained within the single phrase, Myoho-renge-kyo. If we believe in that phrase, we shall naturally be granted the same benefits as he was" (MW-1, 64). The practices to attain Buddhahood carried out by Shakyamuni and all Buddhas throughout time and space, and the virtues they acquired as a result, are all contained in Nam-myoho-renge-kyo. Therefore, by embracing the five characters of the Mystic Law, we naturally acquire the benefit of both the practices and the virtues of Shakyamuni and all Buddhas, and are certain to attain Buddhahood. This is the principle "embracing the Gohonzon is in itself enlightenment." It is also termed "attaining Buddhahood in one's present form" and the "immediate attainment of enlightenment."

Nichiren Daishonin says that, for a person who embraces the Mystic Law, "It is not difficult to become a Buddha" (MW-1, 259). Through the Daishonin's teaching, a path leading to Buddhahood has been established for all. Attaining Buddhahood is

Lectures on the "Expedient Means" Chapter • 57

not something that happens in the distant future or somewhere far away. The Daishonin's Buddhism makes it possible for all people to attain Buddhahood in this lifetime.

The teaching "embracing the Gohonzon is in itself enlightenment" represents a revolutionary view of what it means to attain Buddhahood. President Toda said, "In contrast to the Buddhas of the 'Expedient Means' chapter who have practiced for tens of millions of years, we can complete our practice for attaining Buddhahood by simply believing in the Gohonzon and chanting the single phrase Nam-myoho-renge-kyo."

There is immeasurable benefit in chanting Nam-myoho-renge-kyo even just once. Instantaneously, we gain the full benefit acquired by all Buddhas through their practices of many lifetime over an extremely long time. That's how great is the Mystic Law.

According to the conventional Buddhist view, the process of attaining enlightenment is akin to arduously climbing a mountain road toward the peak of Buddhahood in the far distance. By contrast, Nichiren Daishonin's Buddhism is a teaching that enables all people to reach the summit of enlightenment instantaneously. From the state of Buddhahood, we can gaze down on the surrounding mountains far below and survey the spectacular panorama of nature stretching out in all directions.

We can attain this vast state of Buddhahood directly — right now, right where we are. Then we go out in society and tell others of the exhilaration we experience in manifesting this state of life. This practice represents the quintessence of the Daishonin's Buddhism.

Buddhist Practice Means Challenging Ourselves Daily

Yumyo shojin. Myosho fu mon

He has exerted himself bravely and vigorously, and his name is universally known. (LS2, 23)

THIS passage refers to the practices of the Buddhas of the pre–Lotus Sutra teachings and the theoretical teaching, or first half, of the Lotus Sutra. At the same time it also provides us an important guideline in faith.

In the first place, "bravely and vigorously" means with faith. In his "Six-volume Writings" (Rokkan Sho), the twenty-sixth high priest, Nichikan, citing the interpretation, "'Bravely' means to act with courage; 'vigorously' means to use every ounce of one's wisdom," explains that "bravely and vigorously" means to courageously exercise one's powers of faith to the fullest.

Buddhist practice has to be carried out with determination and courage. When we challenge ourselves bravely with the spirit to accomplish "more today than yesterday" and "more tomorrow than today," we are truly practicing.

Without such a brave and vigorous spirit, we cannot break the iron shackles of destiny, nor can we defeat obstacles and devils. Our daily practice of gongyo is a drama of challenging and creating something new in our lives. When we bravely stand up with faith, the darkness of despair and anxiety vanishes from our hearts, and in pours the light of hope and growth. This spirit to stand up courageously is the spirit of faith.

The Buddha Nature Manifests When We Practice With Sincerity and Consistency

FROM the standpoint of the Daishonin's Buddhism, "exert" means to chant daimoku diligently for the happiness of oneself and others. We can exert ourselves in this fashion only if we possess a brave and vigorous spirit.

High Priest Nichikan, citing Miao-lo's interpretation of the term *exert* as meaning "pure" and "continuous," teaches the proper attitude to have in chanting daimoku. He explains that "pure" means unalloyed, and that "continuous" means to practice continuously and unceasingly. In other words, the important thing is that we chant daimoku each day with sincerity and consistency. Only then does it become the practice for polishing our lives and for attaining Buddhahood in this lifetime.

The Daishonin says: "If you exert a hundred million aeons of effort in a single moment of life, the three enlightened properties of the Buddha will appear within you at each moment. Nam-myoho-renge-kyo is the practice of 'exerting' oneself" (GOSHO ZENSHU, P. 790).

In chanting daimoku, we are carrying out the practice of "exerting" ourselves. Therefore, the three enlightened properties, the immeasurable wisdom and compassion of the Buddha, manifest at each moment in the lives of those who possess extremely earnest concern for the Law, and who bravely and tenaciously struggle for its sake. When we have a brave and vigorous spirit of faith, we instantaneously manifest the "mind of the Buddha." This is what "embracing the Gohonzon is in itself enlightenment" means.

Put another way, the Daishonin is saying that those who bravely and vigorously exert themselves in faith are all Buddhas.

A Life of Continuous 'Self-Improvement'

LET us remember that the SGI has greatly developed precisely because we have bravely and vigorously exerted ourselves in faith — that is, with true earnestness.

Once when asked by a foreign journalist to explain the reason for our great development, I said, "It's because of our wholehearted dedication." The present tremendous advance of kosen-rufu has come about because we have earnestly and wholeheartedly taken action for the sake of friends, society and peace.

A youth once asked Soka Gakkai founding president Tsunesaburo Makiguchi how one could develop the ability to judge good and evil. President Makiguchi replied, "If you have the tenacity and courage to practice the world's foremost religion, you will come to understand." He also once said: "You must bravely and vigorously exert yourself. You must take action. Even though I am now an old man, I, too, am practicing in this manner."

"Exerting oneself bravely and vigorously" truly is the wellspring of the Soka Gakkai spirit. When we bravely challenge ourselves through faith, our lives stir, wisdom is born, our beings overflow with joy and hope.

A person of bravery and vigor who continually, moment by moment, makes causes for self-improvement is an eternal victor. Those who struggle with earnestness and broad-mindedness, with the spirit of a lion king, are certainly exerting brave and vigorous effort.

Shine As a 'Celebrity of the Mystic Law'

THE next line, "his name is universally known," means that the names of those who bravely and vigorously exert themselves in their practice will be known far and wide. Because of their brave and vigorous efforts, they win renown. Because of their splendid Buddhist practice, they move the hearts of all Buddhas.

The Daishonin writes to a follower whose husband is seriously ill:

> No matter what might befall him on the road between this life and the next, he should declare himself to be a disciple of Nichiren.... My name has reached the pure lands of the ten directions, and heaven and earth surely know of it. If your husband declares that he is Nichiren's disciple, no evil demon can possibly claim ignorance of the name. (MW-5, 281-82)

President Toda often told us that when we go to Eagle Peak, we should proudly declare ourselves "disciples of Josei Toda, the leader of kosen-rufu." The names of those who bravely and vigorously dedicate themselves to kosen-rufu are known to all Buddhas and bodhisattvas in the ten directions, and to Bonten and Taishaku and all Buddhist gods. Their reputation extends throughout the universe.

The reason for this, the sutra explains, is that spreading the correct Buddhist teaching in the latter Day of the Law is the most difficult undertaking there is. Accordingly, the great achievement of those who actually spread the Lotus Sutra cannot fail to be known to the beings in the worlds of the ten directions. Therefore, all Buddhas, bodhisattvas and Buddhist gods in the three existences and the ten directions are sure to protect the courageous men and women who propagate the Mystic Law.

In "Emergence of the Treasure Tower," the eleventh chapter of the Lotus Sutra, Shakyamuni says: "This sutra is hard to uphold; if one can uphold it even for a short while [after I have entered extinction] I will surely rejoice and so will the other Buddhas. A person who can do this wins the admiration of the Buddhas" (LS11, 180–81)

And Nichiren Daishonin says: "Now you must build your reputation as a votary of the Lotus Sutra and devote yourself to it" (MW-1, 93); and, "Bring forth the great power of faith and establish your reputation among all the people of Kamakura and the rest of Japan as 'Shijo Kingo of the Hokke sect'" (MW-2 [2ND ED.], 201).

The Daishonin's intent is for each person to shine as a "celebrity of the Mystic Law" in the community and in society. By making dedicated efforts in faith, we are certain to develop such a reputation.

To win a name for oneself through dedication to the Lotus Sutra is the highest honor. The names of those who struggle for kosen-rufu alongside the original Buddha, Nichiren Daishonin, bloom with an eternal fragrance. They are definitely known to all Buddhas in the ten directions.

The ideals and the movement of the SGI have now spread throughout the world, and as a result, voices far and wide are extolling the worth of Buddhism. This might be seen as corroborating the words, "his name is universally known."

This propagation, which has brought the Mystic Law to as many as 115 countries and territories, is certainly without precedent in the history of Buddhism. You, the millions of friends who have emerged from the earth, have accomplished this sacred undertaking. No other individuals or groups have dedicated themselves to spreading Buddhism and elevating the Law with such earnestness.

Your names and the name of the SGI will definitely shine with a golden light in the human history, and also resound throughout the universe, reaching the ears of all Buddhas in the ten directions. This is clear in light of the principle "his name is universally known."

6 – The Daishonin Established the 'Object of Worship Never Known Before'

Joju jinjin. Mi-zo-u ho.

He has realized the Law that is profound and never known before,... (LS2, 23-24)

All People Are Entities of the Mystic Law

ACCORDING to this passage, the Mystic Law in which we believe is the supreme teaching that has "never been known before." When I read these words, I feel as though the dawn were spreading before my eyes.

In the past, Shakyamuni served countless Buddhas and carried out an immeasurable number of religious practices. This passage says that as a result of his arduous practice for enlightenment over a period of countless kalpas, he "has realized the Law that is profound and never known before."

T'ien-t'ai explains that "profound" means "reaching the very foundation of enlightenment." And "never known before" indicates that until then, no one had known of this Law, and that Shakyamuni himself hadn't known of it until he attained enlightenment.

It was therefore certainly beyond the ken of the people of the nine worlds, including the people of the two vehicles and the bodhisattvas. That's why a little later in "Expedient Means" Shakyamuni says, "[The true entity of all phenomena] can only be understood and shared between Buddhas" (LS2, 24). In other words, it is a Law that can only be comprehended by Buddhas.

The Lotus Sutra Makes Public the 'Secret Teaching' for Attaining Buddhahood

THE Lotus Sutra is the teaching that reveals this "Law...never known before," this Law that "can only be understood and shared between Buddhas."

The pre-Lotus Sutra teachings were all expounded "according to others' minds" (*zuitai*), that is, according to the capacities of the people of the nine worlds. For the people of the nine worlds, therefore, the Lotus Sutra is a teaching they have never before heard; and in this sense, too, it is a Law "never known before."

The Lotus Sutra makes public to all people the "secret teaching" "understood and shared [only] between Buddhas" that has never been known before. A genuine "secret teaching" is not something kept to oneself, hidden from others and used to create an aura of mystery or to appropriate authority to oneself.

66 • Daisaku Ikeda

The Nikken sect's authoritarianism is evidence that they totally fail to understand the heart of the Lotus Sutra.

When the proper "time" arrives, a genuine "secret teaching" should be expounded vociferously and spread to cure the ills of all humankind and its brilliant force thus proven. That is the purpose of this "secret teaching," of this "Law that is profound and never known before."

In many Gosho, Nichiren Daishonin refers to the Gohonzon of the Three Great Secret Laws as a "great mandala that has never before been known." In one place, he says: "Even in the Lotus Sutra Shakyamuni only revealed it (the Gohonzon) in the 'Life Span' chapter; and in the 'Supernatural Powers' (Jinriki) chapter he entrusted it to the Bodhisattvas of the Earth" (MW-3, 64-65).

In another place, he states:

> After the Buddha's death, in the two thousand years of the Former and Middle Days of the Law, not even the term "object of worship of the essential teaching" was mentioned, let alone the object itself being inscribed.... T'ien-t'ai, Miao-lo and Dengyo...never expounded it.... Nichiren was the first to inscribe this great mandala. (MW-1, 211)

Nichiren Daishonin bestowed upon all people of the Latter Day of the Law the great "secret teaching" known only to Buddhas in the form of the "object of worship that has never before been known." And toward that end he underwent great persecutions.

It is important to bear in mind the Daishonin's immense compassion as revealed by his actions to spread this teaching. And for the same reason, it is important to practice faith based on a profound sense of gratitude and joy.

The "Law that is profound and never known before" manifests in our lives when we have ardent faith in the "great mandala that has never before been known."

Advance With the Pride of Bodhisattvas of the Earth Creating a New Dawn of Human History

PRESIDENT Toda explained the passage "He has realized the Law that is profound and never known before," as follows: "This refers to the establishment of the Dai-Gohonzon of the Buddhism of sowing in Nichiren Daishonin's own life."

The "Law that is profound and never known before" does not exist somewhere else. It manifests in the living bodies, the actual lives of us [who embrace the Gohonzon]. In the well-known Gosho "On the Treasure Tower," the Daishonin says, "Those who chant Nam-myoho-renge-kyo, irrespective of social status, are themselves Treasure Tower and likewise they themselves are Taho Buddha" (MW-1, 30).

We should erect the Treasure Tower of Nam-myoho-renge-kyo within our lives, he is saying. This is the spirit that imbues the passage "He has realized the Law that is profound and never known before."

Not only Shakyamuni, but all people can awaken to the "Law that is profound and never known before." All people can establish the Treasure Tower in their lives and shine brilliantly as entities of the Treasure Tower. In time, the earth will teem with countless shining Treasure Towers of life. From the standpoint of the Daishonin's Buddhism, this will constitute the actual proof of the passage "He has realized the Law that is profound and never known before." We are opening an unprecedented dawn in human history by means of the great and unprecedented Mystic Law.

Because it is a teaching never known before, votaries and courageous Bodhisattvas of the Earth never known before must appear in order to spread it. President Toda said, "We are members of the Soka Gakkai family, Bodhisattvas of the Earth, who have emerged from the earth to accomplish the unprecedented widespread propagation of the Law." We have inherited President Toda's spirit and are striving to carry out this "practice never known before."

Please be confident that in advancing this "unprecedented movement of kosen-rufu," we will receive immeasurable and boundless good fortune and blessings, the likes of which have never been known before.

The SGI Puts the Daishonin's Intention Into Practice

Zui gi sho setsu. Ishu nange.

...and [he] preaches [this Law] in accordance with what is appropriate, yet his intention is difficult to understand. (LS2, 24)

IN this passage, Shakyamuni explains why the "door to the wisdom" of the Buddhas is difficult to understand and difficult to enter.

Shakyamuni indicates that the pre-Lotus Sutra teachings were expounded according to the various capacities of the people of the nine worlds, and that he has not yet explained his intention — that is, the Buddha's true intention in expounding his teaching — and that no one has yet comprehended it.

It is no simple matter to directly expound the "Law that is profound and never known before," which the Buddha has attained as the result of bold practice. That's because the difference in level of understanding between the Buddha and other beings is so great.

Even were the Buddha to expound the true teaching, should the people's understanding be incomplete, there would be the danger they would develop doubt, destroy the Law and fall into the three evil paths of existence.

Shakyamuni, immediately after attaining the Way beneath the Bodhi tree, at first hesitated to expound the Law. However, he realized that unless he expounded his teaching right then and there, people would be forever locked in the darkness of delusion. Herein lay the inner conflict of Shakyamuni, who pioneered the Way for the enlightenment of all human beings. Overcoming his dilemma, he began to expound the Law.

So that people could gain a correct and unerring understanding of the Law, Shakyamuni, exercising every ounce of his wisdom, continuously pondered how he could convey his enlightenment to as many people as possible. He taxed his ingenuity. Such was Shakyamuni's compassion. Wisdom is born of compassion.

The teachings for people of the three vehicles (of Learning, Realization and Bodhisattva) certainly were set forth according to the people's various capacities. The Buddha expounded the way of the voice-hearers, the way of the *pratyekabuddhas*, and the way of the bodhisattvas, tailoring each teaching to the understanding of each of these groups. In this way, he enabled them to arrive at the "door to the wisdom" of the Buddhas. This was the expedient purpose of the provisional teachings that preceded the Lotus Sutra.

In this passage, Shakyamuni says that he "preaches it in accordance with what is appropriate." In other words, he expounds the Law in accordance with what is appropriate to the capacities of the people.

The Buddha's true intention was always to expound the supreme vehicle of Buddhahood, the path for all people to become Buddhas. However, the voice-hearers and the *pratyekabuddhas* do not understand this. Having grown attached to provisional teachings, they fail to understand that the Buddha's true intention is to enable all people without exception to become Buddhas. They do not comprehend the true teaching that makes all people Buddhas. This is the meaning of "his intention is difficult to understand."

Needless to say, the Buddha did not go out of his way to make his preaching difficult to understand. Rather, the Buddha's intention is difficult to understand because of the disbelief and the attachments of those who receive his teaching.

When people's hearts are closed, they cannot readily accept even sound reasoning. This suggests just how fearful is attachment to mistaken ideas. Such attachment can destroy a person's life.

In fact, the three powerful enemies persecute the Lotus Sutra's votaries precisely because, failing to understand the heart of the Lotus Sutra ("his intention is difficult to understand"), they remain attached to provisional teachings. The sutra says, "The evil monks of that muddied age, failing to understand the Buddha's expedient means, how he preaches the Law in accordance with what is appropriate, will confront us with foul language." (LS13, 195)

Evil priests of the muddied Latter Day of the Law, failing to understand that the teachings expounded before the Lotus Sutra are all "expedient means" taught "in accordance with what is appropriate," become attached to these shallow teachings. As a result, they bear malice toward and persecute the votaries of the Lotus Sutra, who refute the teachings they uphold.

Those who fail to understand and who distort the Buddha's true intention will persecute those who practice exactly as the Buddha taught. And in any age, the former will be numerous and the latter few.

The Shout of Justice, the Victory of the True Teaching

IN a polluted and evil society, those who persecute the votaries of the Lotus Sutra will spread malicious rumors and try to turn public opinion against the votaries. And they will seek to drive off people of justice.

Since this is a muddied world of such inverted proprieties, we need to raise the cry of truth and justice persistently. We must win and show proof of the correct teaching.

After the Daishonin died, his correct teaching was protected because Nikko Shonin stood up alone. Had Nikko Shonin remained silent, then no doubt a history of the "justice of the five senior priests" would have emerged. Instead, Nikko Shonin strictly refuted the erroneous teachings of the five senior priests.

The five senior priests did not understand the Daishonin's "intention," the true intention of the original Buddha. The Daishonin's sole intention was to accomplish the widespread propagation of the object of worship of the Three Great Secret Laws and enable all people of the Latter Day of the Law to become happy.

The five senior priests lost sight of the spirit of the Daishonin, who revealed the Three Great Secret Laws. Nikko Shonin alone followed and served the Daishonin continually, endured persecutions together with him and boldly developed propagation of his teaching in strict accordance with the mentor's instructions. Because he struggled at one in spirit with the mentor, he understood the Daishonin's intention.

You can tell whether the spirit of the mentor has been handed down correctly by looking at the conduct of the disciple. No matter how people may claim to uphold the Three Great Secret Laws, if they are not taking action for kosen-rufu out of the desire for the happiness of all people, then we can only conclude that they have lost sight of the Daishonin's intention.

Seven hundred years after the Daishonin's struggle to spread the teaching in the face of persecution, when his spirit was truly on the verge of becoming extinguished, the Soka Gakkai appeared. The Soka Gakkai is a body that has directly inherited his true teaching and that advances in accord with his will and decree.

The SGI, which is directly connected to the Daishonin, and which thoroughly bases itself on the Gohonzon and the Gosho, is the only body of harmoniously united believers who are correctly passing on what the Daishonin intended.

As glorious "verifiers of the correct teaching," let us speak out for kosen-rufu with lofty pride and dignity and with golden eloquence, not begrudging our voices.

'If We Do Not Harbor Doubts in Our Hearts' We Can Definitely Attain the Summit of Happiness

PRESIDENT Toda explained the meaning of the line "his intention is difficult to understand" as it applies to our practice:

> Whereas the Buddha sees what is to come, for us the future is totally dark, and we can only see what has already passed. For this reason, it is difficult for us to awaken to the heart of the Gohonzon. It is enough that we believe wholeheartedly in the Gohonzon, no matter what. If we do so, then we will definitely receive benefit. It is no good if we start doubting along the way.

He is discussing the ultimate meaning of faith. Firm faith in the Gohonzon leads to the highest "wisdom." This is the principle of "substituting faith for wisdom."

Nichiren Daishonin's intent is to enable all people to become Buddhas. Therefore, it is impossible that those who embrace his Buddhism throughout their lives could fail to realize true happiness.

In the course of our practice, however, various things arise on account of the negative causes and tendencies in our own lives. There may be times when we think, "What did I do to deserve this?" But we should not be swayed every time some such phenomena arise; for it is already certain that we will become happy in the end. We should regard everything that happens to us in our practice to reach the destination of happiness as our training. If we do so, then later on we will see the profound "meaning" and "intention" underlying each of these phenomena.

The Daishonin says, "If we do not harbor doubts in our hearts, we will as a matter of course attain Buddhahood" (MW-2 [2ND ED.], 180). Those who avoid succumbing to doubts no matter what happens are winners in faith. They are people who truly understand the Daishonin's intention.

7—Expedient Means Are Words of Wisdom for Raising People Up

Shari-hotsu. Go ju jo-butsu irai. Shuju innen. Shuju hiyu. Ko en gonkyo. Mu shu hoben. Indo shujo. Ryo ri sho jaku.

"Shariputra, ever since I attained Buddhahood I have through various causes and various similes widely expounded my teachings and have used countless expedient means to guide living beings and cause them to renounce their attachments. (LS2, 24)

HERE, Shakyamuni is elaborating on the immediately preceding passage, where he says, "He [a Buddha] has realized the Law that is profound and never known before, and preaches it in accordance with what is appropriate [to the capacities of the people], yet his intention is difficult to understand."

Shakyamuni had earlier discussed the "wisdom of the Buddhas." In this passage, by contrast, he reveals this wisdom as he has gathered it up in himself.

"Ever since I attained Buddhahood" refers to the period from when Shakyamuni attained enlightenment until he taught the Lotus Sutra, during which time he expounded various provisional sutras. Shakyamuni then clarifies the distinctive character of the pre-Lotus Sutra teachings. He says that before teaching the Lotus Sutra he had employed "various causes" (explaining why things are the way they are) and "various similes" in widely expounding his teaching; and that these teachings were "expedient means" (*hoben*) for guiding people to the truth and freeing them from their various attachments.

The Expedient Means of the Pre-Lotus Sutra Teachings

AN expedient means is a means or a device that the Buddha, out of compassion, employs to help people attain enlightenment. From the outset, Shakyamuni's ultimate purpose lay in enabling all people to attain Buddhahood; but he did not reveal this in the provisional sutras. He reveals it for the first time in the Lotus Sutra.

The purpose of the provisional sutras is to enable people to part with various attachments. People differ in terms of the types of attachments or "fetters" they possess. Therefore, Shakyamuni expounded a variety of teachings, employing various causes and similes that matched the capacities of specific people.

These teachings were all no more than "means" for drawing people toward the "end" of attaining Buddhahood. In this sense, the pre-Lotus Sutra teachings are regarded as expedient means.

Still, the expedient teachings expounded before the Lotus Sutra also arose from the Buddha's compassion. Shakyamuni strove to respond to the different capacities of people, to select teachings that precisely matched their needs, and to satisfy everyone. He was waging a struggle of compassion and wisdom.

"What is this person seeking?" "How should I instruct this person to ensure that he or she will not deviate from the correct path?" He deeply considered the case of each individual, and gave instruction with an earnest "must-win" spirit.

Though we may speak of "the people" in the aggregate, they are not an abstract, homogeneous multitude; they are not a colorless mass. "How can the heart of this person before me be opened?" "How can I reinvigorate this specific individual?" This is the spirit of Buddhism. When speaking to a large number of people, only if we have the attitude of addressing each individual can we offer "living words" that reverberate in the hearts of many.

Since attaining the Way, Shakyamuni thoroughly devoted himself to expounding the Law for the sake of individuals. Because his words and phrases were uttered for individuals and with their happiness in mind, the Law imbued the life of one person after another. Because he waged such a struggle, he sent people's hearts a fresh breeze, dispelling the dark clouds of doubt and anxiety and causing the sun of hope and happiness to rise. Because he regarded the individual with such warmth, people from all walks of life — young and old, men and women — gathered with joy and enthusiasm to hear Shakyamuni expound his teachings.

Shakyamuni preached the expedient teachings because he sympathized with the people, whose lives were steeped in illusion and suffering. He was impelled by the desire to somehow help them. This led him to consider, "By what means can I save them from suffering?" "How might I liberate them from illusion?" In other words, expedients arose from his desire to help people; his compassion gave birth to wisdom.

Shakyamuni, who attained enlightenment beneath the Bodhi tree, aroused a spirit of great mercy and determined to save all people from suffering. At that time, the Buddhas of the ten directions appeared and urged Shakyamuni on, saying: "Following the example of all other Buddhas, you will employ the power of expedient means. We too...make distinctions and preach the three vehicles" (LS2, 43). Thereupon Shakyamuni, preparatory to expounding the Law "never known before" to which he had become enlightened, began to expound the pre-Lotus Sutra teachings using the power of expedient means.

Expedient means are expressions of wisdom serving to raise people up. Shakyamuni, armed with words of compassion and wisdom, thus resolutely took the first step on the difficult journey to expound the Law for the salvation of all people. And so he raised the curtain on Buddhism, which sends out a message of happiness to all humankind.

The 'Secret and Mystic Expedient' of the Lotus Sutra

AS I have already mentioned, the "expedient means" to which this passage refers are the expedient means of the pre-Lotus Sutra teachings. These are not to be confused with the expedient means indicated by the title of the second chapter of the Lotus Sutra. Profound significance is attached to the expedient means of the Lotus Sutra.

T'ien-t'ai identifies three types of expedient means: "functional-teaching expedients," "truth-gateway expedients" and the "secret and mystic expedient." The first two correspond to the expedient means of the pre-Lotus Sutra teachings. The secret and mystic expedient corresponds to the expedient means of the Lotus Sutra, the expedient means of the "Expedient Means" chapter.

Functional-teaching expedients (*hoyu hoben*) are the various teachings expounded according to the differing capacities of the people. Through the function (*yu*) of these teachings (*ho*) Shakyamuni brought benefit to people of various capacities.

Truth-gateway expedients (*notsu hoben*) are teachings that represent the gateway for entering the truth. To follow these teachings is termed *notsu*, because through them people are led to the truth.

These expedients of the pre-Lotus Sutra teachings serve to guide people to the wisdom of the Buddha; they are "means" for directing people until they have reached the Lotus Sutra. And, as Shakyamuni indicates when he says "honestly discarding expedient means," (LS2, 44) the expedients of the pre-Lotus Sutra teachings should be discarded once the Lotus Sutra has been expounded.

Shakyamuni Dared To Express the Truth in Words

BY contrast, the expedient of the Lotus Sutra is not an expedient that ought to be discarded; it is the teaching of the truth. At the same time, however, it is still always just an expedient. Although the second chapter explains the truth, it is titled not "Truth" but "Expedient Means." Herein lies the profound significance of the secret and mystic expedient (*himyo hoben*).

In the opening of "Expedient Means," we are told that the wisdom of the Buddhas is infinitely profound and immeasurable, and difficult for all voice-hearers and *pratyekabuddhas* to comprehend. It is the ultimate teaching that defies expression through words and so cannot be explained.

However, unless the wisdom of all Buddhas is expressed, all people will forever remain shut away in darkness. For this reason, the Buddha ventures to put it into words.

Compared with the inexpressible truth, the words the Buddha uses to expound it are an expedient. At the same time, however, it is a fact that through these words people can be saved. The words of the Lotus Sutra that the Buddha, out of his compassion, expounded "according with his own mind" for all people, constitute the secret and mystic expedient; more than simply a means, the words are an expedient at one with the Buddha's wisdom.

Regarding the words of the Lotus Sutra, Nichiren Daishonin says things like: "Its words are the reality of life" (MW-1, 3); "Each of the 69,384 characters of the Lotus Sutra is a Buddha" (*GOSHO ZENSHU*, P. 971); and "When you cast your eyes upon the words of the Lotus Sutra, you should consider that you are beholding the living body of the Buddha Shakyamuni" (MW-5, 147). The Daishonin thus repeatedly emphasizes the oneness of the Buddha's wisdom and the words whereby it is expressed.

In a sense, it could be said that the expedients of the pre-Lotus Sutra teachings and the expedient of the Lotus Sutra are entirely opposite in their directionality. The Japanese term *hoben* (expedient means) originally derives from the Sanskrit *upaya*, meaning "approach." The pre-Lotus Sutra teachings enable people to move away from illusion and approach enlightenment. The direction, in other words, is toward the wisdom of the Buddhas. This is the direction of the functional-teaching expedients and the truth-gateway expedients. These expedients are no longer of any use once we arrive at the teaching of the Lotus Sutra.

In the Lotus Sutra, by contrast, Shakyamuni explains and articulates the wisdom of the Buddhas — to the world and in a manner according with his own mind. The directionality of this expedient is thus that of the Buddha approaching the world of human beings. This is the secret and mystic expedient.

Through the power of the Lotus Sutra, pre-Lotus Sutra teachings take on importance as partial expressions of the truth. They are said to be "revealed and unified" in the teaching of the Lotus Sutra.

Revealing the Power of the Mystic Law Through Our Struggles

THE wisdom of the Buddhas revealed in the "Expedient Means" chapter is the "true entity of all phenomena." Put another way, it is the truth that all living beings are Buddhas.

The "secret" of the secret and mystic expedient is that this truth can only be understood between Buddhas. It is called "mystic" because it is difficult for people to comprehend. The teaching that awakens people to the truth that all living beings are Buddhas is the secret and mystic expedient.

This is exemplified in the parable of the gem in the robe related in "Prophecy of Enlightenment for Five Hundred Disciples" (Gohyaku Deshi Juki), the eighth chapter of the Lotus Sutra: A man is given a priceless gem by a close friend, who sews it into the lining of his robe while he drowses in a drunken stupor. Not realizing he possesses the gem, the man suffers hardships and is always in want. Much later he meets the friend again, and only then does he discover that all along he has had the gem of great value.

The man's friend (the Buddha) knew that the man possessed the gem in his robe (the world of Buddhahood in his life), even though the man (representing the beings of the nine worlds) failed to realize it.

An ordinary human being is a Buddha. This is difficult to understand. Unless we believe we possess the Buddha nature, it will remain forever "secret." However, once we recognize it, it is no longer "secret," and our "mystic" powers appear.

The second Soka Gakkai president, Josei Toda, said: "That we are merely ordinary, unenlightened beings is the secret and mystic expedient. The truth is that we are Buddhas." To realize this truth is to understand the secret and mystic expedient.

Although we are Buddhas, we are born as common mortals. This is so that, through doing our human revolution and showing proof of the Mystic Law, we can accomplish kosen-rufu. If we had everything, including good health and riches, from the outset, then other people could not understand the power of the Mystic Law. Therefore, we try to reveal it to them through our struggles as common mortals. This is the secret and mystic expedient.

Victory in Life Through Victory in Faith

IN a word, all of us who believe in the Gohonzon, the Lotus Sutra of the Latter Day of the Law, and who are struggling amid the reality of the nine worlds exemplify the secret and mystic expedient.

As long as we always live based on the Gohonzon, then any and all sufferings become expedient means for us to strengthen and deepen the world of Buddhahood in our lives. Sufferings and joys and everything that happens to us become expedient means for us to reveal the power of the Mystic Law.

It is said that life is like a drama. Whether in the world of business, education, the home or wherever, each person acts out a drama. This "role" is itself an expedient means; but should the "actor" abandon this role, he or she will be at a loss for a mission. When acting out our respective roles, we manifest our own inner truth most fully.

Daily life equals faith. And the world of Buddhahood appears nowhere except wedded to the stage of the reality of the nine worlds. Let us enact the drama of human revolution on the stage of our lives.

From misery to happiness, from disappointment to hope, from fate to mission, from suffering to eternal joy — the driving force that makes these dynamic transformations possible is the Mystic Law, is faith.

8 — The Buddha Struggles To Change People's Hearts Through Dialogue

Shari-hotsu. Go ju jo-butsu irai. Shuju innen. Shuju hiyu. Ko en gonkyo. Mu shu hoben. Indo shujo. Ryo ri sho jaku.

"Shariputra, ever since I attained Buddhahood I have through various causes and various similes widely expounded my teachings and have used countless expedient means to guide living beings and cause them to renounce their attachments. (LS2, 24)

Lectures on the "Expedient Means" Chapter • 85

DIALOGUE is the lifeline of Buddhism. The Buddha's fundamental objective is to develop in the lives of all people a wisdom equal to his own.

As this implies, we tell others about Buddhism because, fundamentally, we venerate their lives. If, on the other hand, we had the attitude, "Even if I tell this person about Buddhism, it couldn't possibly do any good," then we simply would not bother talking to them.

We tell people about Buddhism because we respect them as human beings. Because we trust the person, we can conduct tenacious dialogue.

Saying, "I have... widely expounded my teachings and have used countless expedient means to guide living beings," Shakyamuni indicates that he has guided people through free and boundless dialogue. Shakyamuni and Nichiren Daishonin both spread the Law through talking and speaking out in the very midst of the people.

Josei Toda and Tsunesaburo Makiguchi, the first and second presidents of the Soka Gakkai, were also experts at dialogue and discussion. Regardless of the social standing of the person they were addressing, they always spoke with dignity and conviction. They created a history of such conversation.

The power of dialogue changes people's hearts. Sincere dialogue is the sunlight that can soften and melt hearts that are thoroughly frozen over. Clear, confident words are the fresh breeze that dispels clouds of illusion. Buddhist dialogue is the prime point for bringing change to people's lives.

Shakyamuni says here that he has conducted compassionate dialogue and spoken earnestly with a "must-win" spirit in order to help others; and that he has exercised every ounce of wisdom and ingenuity to ensure that his words might reach people's hearts. This is the significance of the "various causes and various similes" to which he refers. In other words, he continually spoke out and conducted dialogue, explaining the reason behind the unfolding of actions and events and employing examples to make his teaching easy to understand.

The 'Cause' To Dedicate One's Life to Kosen-rufu

IN Japan today, the word *innen* (causes) is often associated with the curses of the spirits of deceased ancestors or some such superstition. But this has nothing to do with the original meaning of the term in Buddhism. The causes of our happiness or misfortune all exist within our own lives.

In Buddhism, *innen*, or causes, has a more profound meaning. It includes the ideas of "cause and effect," "origin" and "relation."[1]

One Buddhist scripture, for example, explains the "causes" for King Ashoka as follows. There are two young boys, Tokusho Doji and Musho Doji, who once made offerings to Shakyamuni. Tokusho Doji offers him a mud pie, while Musho Doji presses his palms together in reverence. Shakyamuni then explains to his disciple Ananda, "Tokusho Doji is sure to be reborn as a king

---

1. *innen* (Skt. *hetu-pratyaya*): This term is a compound of the two units *in* and *en*. In terms of the ten factors of life expounded in the "Expedient Means" chapter, *in* (or *nyo ze in*) means internal cause, and *en* (*nyo ze en*) means external cause or relation. According to Buddhist doctrine, everything happens as a result of the interplay of *in* and *en*, or internal and external causes.

Lectures on the "Expedient Means" Chapter • 87

named Ashoka." Later, according to traditional accounts, Tokusho Doji, due to the causes he formed in making an offering to the Buddha, is born as the son of King Bindusara named Ashoka.

In the pre-Lotus Sutra teachings, through examples such as these, Shakyamuni strove to help people awaken to the strict law of cause and effect operating in their lives.

When We Remember Our Mission, We Can Manifest Our True Ability and Win

STILL greater significance attaches to the "causes" expounded in the Lotus Sutra. These concern what might be termed the life-to-life bond between the Buddha and the people; the relationship that has existed between the Buddha and living beings since the remote past of *sanzen-jintengo* or *gohyaku-jintengo*.

In this connection, President Toda discussed "various causes" from the standpoint of the Daishonin's Buddhism as follows:

> Regarding the meaning of "various causes": in the time of *kuon ganjo* we were followers of the original Buddha Nichiren Daishonin. Because of this "cause," now in the Latter Day of the Law, more than 600 years after the Daishonin's passing, as disciples of Nichiren Daishonin, we have appeared in Japan, a country steeped in misery, as poor people. And we demonstrate that by believing in this Gohonzon, we can become wealthy. When we recall the cause we made in having promised to accomplish kosen-rufu, our poverty and other sufferings will vanish in an instant.

To prove the power of benefit of the Mystic Law, we need to experience various worries and struggles in our present existence. Having promised in the primal moment of *kuon ganjo* to accomplish the widespread propagation of the Mystic Law, we have now been born to carry out this mission.

It is impossible that a Bodhisattva of the Earth could remain submerged in suffering or be defeated by hardships. Once we realize the cause — namely, that we were born in our circumstances in accordance with our own wishes in order to prove the validity of Buddhism — we can definitely win.

One Person's Victory Provides an Illustration for All

NEXT, "various similes" in this passage refers to the allegories and parables Shakyamuni expounded in the pre-Lotus Sutra teachings. Using natural reason and examples from immediate life experience to explain difficult Buddhist principles makes them easy to understand. This is Shakyamuni's purpose in employing similes.

The use of similes, therefore, arises from compassion for others. Precisely because the Buddha's spirit of compassion is so strong, he expounds skillful similes in hopes of making his teachings as easy as possible to understand.

The Buddha, adapting his preaching to the people's capacity, draws comparisons with a wide variety of natural phenomena and common observations. For example, in the pre-Lotus Sutra teachings, he variously compares earthly desires to a fierce current that carries people along, to a shade that conceals the light of the Buddha nature, to flames that consume one's body and mind, to poison that harms one greatly, and to a dense forest where those who become lost can never find their way out. In this way, he taught people the fearfulness of, and tried to cause them to renounce, earthly desires.

Simply renouncing earthly desires, however, does not amount to attaining the enlightenment of the Buddha. The similes of the pre-Lotus Sutra teachings explain the Buddha's wisdom from one angle only. In fact, there is the danger that if we become overly preoccupied with these similes, it will actually increase the difficulty of attaining Buddhahood.

By contrast, the similes of the Lotus Sutra are at one with the Buddha's wisdom. That's because they reveal and express the Buddha's enlightenment and wisdom just as it is.

Composing Various Similes of Actual Proof

MOREOVER, viewed from the standpoint of the fundamental law of Nam-myoho-renge-kyo, it might be said that all sutras, including the twenty-eight-chapter Lotus Sutra, are grand similes to help people understand the Gohonzon of Nam-myoho-renge-kyo.

From the standpoint of the Daishonin's Buddhism, instances of actual proof of faith manifesting in our daily lives are also similes explaining the Gohonzon's power of benefit. These similes of actual proof in daily life are in fact eloquent testimony to the truth of the Gohonzon.

Regarding "various similes," President Toda explained that the life-or-death struggles to propagate the Law undertaken by followers who were the Daishonin's contemporaries, and the abundant benefit they received, serve as similes for us in modern times.

The outstanding activities of the Daishonin's followers in his day provide an example for those of later ages. There is Shijo Kingo, who overcame hardships in his place of work; the Ikegami brothers, who brought their father — who had opposed their teaching — to convert to the Daishonin's teaching; Nanjo Tokimitsu, who defeated the devil of illness and dedicated his life to the mission of a successor; Myoichi-ama, who struggled in the cause of faith for herself and on behalf of her deceased husband; and the list goes on and on. The actual proof of each follower of the Daishonin who overcame difficult circumstances is a source of great encouragement for us as we face similar problems in our own lives.

This same basic principle applies to our discussion of our own experiences. One person's victorious experience can provide courage, hope and heartfelt understanding to many others.

Our victories become splendid illustrations of how many others can win. Our triumphs over hardships provide many others with the confidence: "If that's the case, then I can win, too. That person can win, too. Everyone can be victorious."

When talking about the power of the Mystic Law, people may discuss your victory as a "simile," saying, "Just look at him, for example," or "Look at the human revolution she is carrying out."

In this sense, let us compose many dramas of human revolution for the sake of others. Let us adorn our lives with many "various causes" and "various similes."

Lectures on the "Expedient Means" Chapter • 91

And let us decorate our communities like flower gardens filled with the "various similes" of many and varied dramas of human revolution, with one person after another realizing victory and becoming happy.

The Wisdom to Discern the True Nature of Attachments

SHAKYAMUNI says that he tried to free people from various desires and illusions by employing various causes and similes.

The fundamental cause of people's unhappiness lies in their tendency to develop attachments of various kinds. An attachment, just as it sounds, is a fetter on one's heart; it indicates earthly desires, cravings and the like. In the pre-Lotus Sutra teachings, Shakyamuni taught the people of the nine worlds, whose lives were steeped in misery, the path for freeing themselves from such attachments. That is, as he says in the above passage, he "caused them to renounce their attachments."

The spirit of the Lotus Sutra, however, is not to eradicate earthly desires. When we base ourselves on the Mystic Law, we can transform desires — just as they are — into enlightenment. This is the principle of "earthly desires are enlightenment."

Regarding the passage in "Former Affairs of the Bodhisattva Medicine King," the twenty-third chapter, "[The Lotus Sutra] can cause living beings to cast off all...pain," (LS23, 286) Nichiren Daishonin says in the "Ongi Kuden" (Record of the Orally Transmitted Teachings) that "cast off" should be interpreted as meaning "become enlightened concerning" (*GOSHO ZENSHU*, P. 773).

In terms of the Daishonin's Buddhism, therefore, "cause them to renounce their attachments" should be interpreted as meaning "cause them to become enlightened concerning their attachments." It's not a matter of eradicating attachments but of seeing them clearly. In other words, rather than causing us to abandon our earthly desires and attachments, our Buddhist practice enables us to discern their true nature and utilize them as the driving force to become happy.

The truth is that we could not in fact eradicate our attachments even if we so wished. And if, for the sake of argument, it were feasible, doing so would make it impossible to live in the real world.

What is important is that we make full use of our attachments rather than allow them to control us. Toward that end, it is necessary that we clearly recognize them for what they are.

Make Full Use of Your Attachments

PRESIDENT Toda said:

> The Gohonzon enables us to perceive our attachments just as they are. I believe that each of you has attachments. I, too, have attachments. Because we have attachments, we can lead interesting and significant lives. For example, to succeed in business or to do a lot of shakubuku, we must have attachment to such activities. Our faith enables us to maintain these attachments in such a way that they do not cause us suffering. Rather

than being controlled by our attachments, we need to fully utilize of our attachments to become happy.

The essence of Mahayana Buddhism lies in developing the state of life to clearly discern and thoroughly utilize our attachments, and in leading lives made interesting and significant by cultivating strong attachments.

In short, we should cause the firewood of earthly desires to burn high and, to that same extent, chant sincere daimoku and take action. In so doing, our earthly desires become a springboard to propel us toward our attainment of Buddhahood.

Faith means creating a "mountain" for ourselves and then climbing it; and then starting out again. In this process, we develop from a state of life in which we are caught up with our own small worries, to one in which we can challenge progressively greater worries — for the sake of a friend, for many others, for all humankind.

Toward that end, it is important that we always consider the purpose of our actions. When we clearly establish our fundamental objective in life, we can utilize our attachments most fully and profitably. We can turn them into tailwinds to propel us toward happiness.

This principle offers an extremely valuable gauge for living in modern society, where people are constantly swept along by various wants and cravings.

9 — The Buddha Is a Great Doctor of Life Who Guides People Toward Happiness

Sho-i sha ga. Nyorai hoben. Chiken hara-mitsu. Kai i gu-soku.

Why is this? Because the Thus Come One is fully possessed of both expedient means and the paramita of wisdom. (LS2, 24)

IN this section, Shakyamuni continues to praise the immense wisdom of the Buddha. Until this point, he has praised the Buddha's wisdom from the standpoint of the immeasurable practices that the Buddha carried out in the past. Here he discusses the power of wisdom to guide people and the state of life that the Buddha has attained as a result of these practices.

Knowledge and Wisdom Are Not the Same

CONTINUING from the preceding passage, Shakyamuni now clarifies why the Buddha has used all manner of causes and similes to guide people and have them renounce attachments. And he explains how the Buddha could do this.

In "expedient means and paramita of wisdom," "paramita of wisdom" means the perfection of wisdom. The Sanskrit word *paramita* means "to attain or perfect." Also, "fully possessed" in the above passage means "endowed with." The Buddha, having perfected various practices and attained an extremely profound state of enlightenment, possesses skillful means for guiding people and is endowed with wisdom. For this reason, he can guide people in a way that exactly matches their capacity.

In the section that follows, Shakyamuni explains specifically what he means by wisdom. There he says that the Buddha possesses the powers of wisdom of "immeasurable [mercy], unlimited [eloquence], power, fearlessness" (LS2, 24). I will discuss the contents of this passage in detail in my next lecture. But for the time being, let it suffice to say that these powers are specific functions of wisdom that the Buddha uses to guide people to happiness.

Buddhism is a religion of wisdom. The second Soka Gakkai president, Josei Toda, would often say: "One cause of people's misfortune today is that they confuse knowledge and wisdom.... Knowledge is not wisdom. Knowledge may serve as a door that opens the way to wisdom, but knowledge itself is definitely not wisdom."

For example, taking business administration classes in college doesn't guarantee that you will prosper in the business world. In fact, many people realize commercial success without ever having gone to business school.

Reading many books on child rearing doesn't guarantee that someone can parent well. The truth is that innumerable factors contribute to children's growth. There are even accounts of mothers who become neurotic because in raising their children they encounter situations that completely contradict what they have read in books.

Knowledge is of course necessary. To know something is a great strength. In modern society, in particular, it might be said that knowledge has increasingly come to be used as a weapon. At the same time, merely having some knowledge does not produce value. Happiness cannot be created by knowledge alone. An increase in knowledge definitely does not equal an increase in happiness. The important thing is that people possess the fundamental wisdom to use their knowledge most fully.

To take one example, theories on childhood education often stress the importance of talking to children at their eye-level. Someone with experience in this area comments as follows:

> What should you do when a child starts pleading with you to buy him or her something at a store or somewhere, and then sits down on the floor and cries, refusing to budge until you give in? Under such circumstances, no amount of standing above the child and scolding will do any good. The best approach is to sit down right there together with the child. When you do so, the child, in amazement, will stop crying. And if you then quietly admonish the child, you will find that he or she is surprisingly ready to do as you say.

This method, of course, will not necessarily work every time. Still, it doubtless represents individual wisdom arising from the person's spirit as a parent to connect on a heart-to-heart level with the child. Knowledge of the importance of talking at the child's eye-level produced this kernel of practical wisdom.

'What Purpose Does This Knowledge Serve?'

IN any event, unless we continually ask ourselves "What purpose does this knowledge serve?" we are liable to fall into the trap of pursuing knowledge for its own sake.

To illustrate, the mission of a teacher is to provide instruction. The teacher's purpose is to cultivate the character and wisdom of the pupils and help them acquire skills and abilities they will need to lead happy lives.

This is the purpose of the teacher's knowledge as an educator. But unless the teacher also possesses the wisdom necessary to attain this objective, he or she is not a true educator.

Politicians, as public servants, have the duty to devote themselves selflessly to the happiness and prosperity of the people; and toward that end, they must seek the counsel of many others and work to implement their ideas. If politicians lack the wisdom and power of action to improve society, then they are not true politicians.

The purpose of scholars, likewise, is to contribute to humanity through their academic endeavors.

We need to constantly ask ourselves whether we have realized our fundamental mission, our purpose. If we should forget this and instead gloat arrogantly over how much we know, over our standing or access to information, or over our "vast" knowledge, then our basic spirit will become distorted.

By rights, education, science, politics, economics and all fields of human endeavor exist to serve the happiness of all humanity.

For what purpose, then, did the Buddha appear in the world? His objective, too, was to enable people to become happy; specifically, to enable all people to realize a state of eternal happiness. Thus, there is no contradiction between Buddhism and other areas of human endeavor. Knowledge in all areas yields the greatest value when based on the wisdom of Buddhism.

In the "Expedient Means" chapter, Shakyamuni explains that the Buddha's purpose in appearing in this world is "to open the door of Buddha wisdom to all living beings," "to show the Buddha wisdom to living beings," "to cause living beings to awaken to the Buddha wisdom," and "to induce living beings to enter the path of Buddha wisdom" (LS2, 31). These four aspects of the Buddha wisdom of "opening," "showing," "awakening" and "causing to enter" together are termed the "one great reason" (*ichidaiji innen*) for the Buddha's appearance in the world.

In short, Shakyamuni taught that the path to happiness lies in each person developing his or her own wisdom. The Buddha's wisdom, too, was born of his strong sense of purpose and awareness of his mission.

Tending the Ills of Humankind With the Medicine of the Law

BUDDHISM teaches the supreme way to live.

The question-and-answer sessions President Toda held were truly "forums of wisdom" for leading people to happiness. With great confidence of faith, he candidly gave guidance regarding people's various worries and sufferings in life — from sickness and loss of work to debt and marital problems — hitting the nail on the head every time. Through his encouragement, participants recovered their spirits instantly and became filled with courage and hope.

He would remark: "You know people from how they walk, from how they perk up their shoulders, from their voices. Similarly, from the slightest gesture, from how they open a door, you can tell what their worries are."

A true leader of Buddhism can discern the state of people's lives with such deftness and profundity and can explain the Law to them in a way tailored to their situation.

It is difficult to explain Buddhism correctly, that is, in a manner that accords with the time and people's capacity. There is an account of how even Shariputra blundered in expounding the Law.

Shariputra was once explaining Buddhism to a blacksmith and a laundry man. Shariputra attempted to instruct the blacksmith by teaching him to meditate on the vileness of the body and to instruct the laundryman by teaching him breath-counting meditation. Neither could grasp the teaching, however, and they both developed disbelief. Shariputra ought to have taught the blacksmith to practice breath-counting meditation and the laundryman to meditate on the vileness of the body.

The reason for this is as follows. A blacksmith continually strikes hot iron with a hammer while fanning the fire with a bellows and so constantly works to control the rhythm of his breathing. Had Shariputra explained the breath-counting meditation to the blacksmith, he could have understood it immediately and advanced in his Buddhist practice. Likewise, the work of a laundryman involves cleaning dirty clothes, so had Shariputra taught him to meditate on the vileness of the body, he without doubt could have grasped it.

But Shariputra instructed each in the teaching appropriate to the other. As a result they failed to gain any result. For all of his efforts, Shariputra succeeded only in causing them suffering.

To expound a teaching appropriate to each person is extremely difficult. Nichiren Daishonin established, however, a method of practice accessible to all people regardless of their capacity. Thus he says, "Nam-myoho-renge-kyo is recommended for people of all capacities" (GOSHO ZENSHU, P. 875). And for precisely this reason, the benefit of telling others about the Mystic Law is immense.

A physician of rich experience can grasp a patient's malady accurately and prescribe a treatment that matches the person's

Lectures on the "Expedient Means" Chapter • 101

constitution. Such a physician possesses not only medical knowledge but the wisdom to use that knowledge to the fullest extent. True knowledge is at one with wisdom.

There probably aren't any physicians who would simply tell a patient, "You have appendicitis," without doing anything about it. It might be said that true medical knowledge, or wisdom, lies in curing people of their conditions and returning them to a state of health.

The Buddha is a great "physician of life," who guides all to happiness. The Buddha clearly discerns the fundamental cause of people's suffering and teaches them the path to eternal happiness, how to live a boundlessly fresh and exhilarating life. This is the wisdom of the Buddha.

In this age, when it has become natural for people to lack compassion, no one can match the fellow members of the SGI in bringing a fresh wind of revitalization to many others. There is no other popular organization in the world whose members are so sincere, or who pray and take action as we do for others. There are many eminent people and intellectuals in the world, but I believe that SGI members are even more respectable. You are "doctors" and "nurses" of wisdom worthy of the greatest admiration.

Faith Contains the *Paramita* of Wisdom

HOW do Shariputra and the others gathered at the assembly react when hearing Shakyamuni expound the "Expedient Means" chapter? Do they think, "I couldn't possibly have even an iota of the perfect wisdom of the Buddha in me"?

No. In fact, they say to themselves: "If this teaching represents the wonderful Buddha wisdom that can save people, then I want to learn it, too. I want to make it my own."

In "Expedient Means," Shariputra and the others "wish to hear the teaching of perfect endowment" (LS2, 28). In other words, they arouse a seeking mind for the path leading to the Buddha's state of life, which is "fully possessed of both expedient means and the paramita of wisdom."

Rather than think, "I've heard all I need to hear," they become even more high spirited and encouraged.

In "The Opening of the Eyes," Nichiren Daishonin says that this "teaching of perfect endowment" is Nam-myoho-renge-kyo (MW-2, [2ND ED.] 116).

In the pre-Lotus Sutra teachings, Shakyamuni expounded the six *paramitas* as practices for bodhisattvas to attain the state of life of the Buddha. The idea was that through carrying out the six practices of almsgiving, keeping the precepts, forbearance, assiduousness, meditation and obtaining wisdom, they could approach the state of life of the Buddha. Such a practice, carried out in lifetime after lifetime over a vast period of time, is termed "practicing toward enlightenment over a period of countless kalpas."

However, the Muryogi Sutra, which serves as an introduction to the Lotus Sutra, states [as quoted in a Gosho]: "[If you embrace this sutra,] you will naturally receive the benefits of the six *paramitas* without having to practice them" (MW-1, 63-64). In other words, even though we do not practice the six *paramitas*, by embracing the Lotus Sutra, we are naturally endowed with their benefit.

Believe in the Gohonzon and Advance With the SGI

"DISTINCTIONS in Benefits," the seventeenth chapter of the Lotus Sutra explains that the benefit of those who understand and believe in the Lotus Sutra when they hear it expounded is great beyond measure. It says that their benefit will be a hundred, a thousand, ten thousand, million times greater than the benefit of practicing the five *paramitas* (i.e., excluding the *paramita* of obtaining wisdom) for a period of "eight hundred thousand million nayutas of kalpas" (LS17, 237).

The *paramita* of obtaining wisdom is excluded because this is the fundamental *paramita*; it is in a class by itself in terms of its importance relative to the other five *paramitas*. To put it another way, it might be said that the five *paramitas* are practiced to attain the *paramita* of wisdom. Buddhism always places the greatest importance on wisdom.

Therefore, Nichiren Daishonin says that practitioners in the Latter Day of the Law "who have just aroused aspiration for enlightenment" need not practice the five *paramitas* (MW-6, 218-19). This view of Buddhist practice — expressed at a time when making offerings to priests, upholding the precepts and the other *paramitas* were being promulgated in earnest — represents a great religious revolution.

Moreover, the Daishonin's Buddhism teaches the principle of "substituting faith for wisdom." Correct faith itself becomes wisdom. Through believing in the Gohonzon, we in the Latter Day of the Law can gain the same benefit as we would by carrying out all of the six *paramitas*, including the *paramita* of obtaining wisdom.

In conclusion, those who now believe in the Gohonzon and advance toward kosen-rufu together with the SGI can gain the benefit of the six *paramitas*. Those who persevere in carrying out activities for kosen-rufu with others lead lives of the highest wisdom. The examples of your many seniors in faith attest to this. When we look back on our lives later on, we can see this clearly.

Because we practice faith, let us strive to live most wisely each day based on the principles of "faith manifesting itself in daily life" and "action manifesting itself in good health."

10 — Secure a Great State of Life by Taking Action for Kosen-rufu

Shari-hotsu. Nyorai chiken. Kodai jinnon. Muryo muge. Riki. Mu-sho-i. Zenjo. Gedas. Sanmai. Jin nyu musai. Joju issai. Mi-zo-u ho.

"Shariputra, the wisdom of the Thus Come One is expansive and profound. He has immeasurable [mercy], unlimited [eloquence], power, fearlessness, concentration, emancipation and samadhis, and has deeply entered the boundless and awakened to the Law never before attained. (LS2, 24)

THIS passage explains the expansive powers of the Buddha. That is, it describes the wonderful state of life that those who embrace the Gohonzon can develop.

Interpreting this passage of "Expedient Means" from the standpoint of Nichiren Daishonin's Buddhism, the second Soka Gakkai president, Josei Toda, taught that it explains the state of life [embodied] in the Gohonzon:

> The difference between the state of life of [the Buddha of] Nam-myoho-renge-kyo and that of the Buddha of the theoretical teaching of the Lotus Sutra is as vast as that between heaven and earth. [Just as the sutra says] without our having made the slightest effort, "This cluster of unsurpassed jewels has come to us unsought" (LS4, 87). We are given in its entirety the benefit of all Buddhas throughout the existences of past, present and future.
>
> Even though we have not carried out any practices in the past, by believing in the Gohonzon, our lives become endowed with many, varied powers. And, through the principle of the simultaneity of cause and effect, we enter the world of Buddhahood just as we are — as ordinary people.

From the standpoint of the Daishonin's Buddhism, these powers are all attributes of the state of life of the Gohonzon. These powers well forth in our own lives when we carry through with our faith. What a wonderful teaching this is.

The Functions of Buddhahood in Our Lives

HERE, Shakyamuni identifies "immeasurable mercy," "unlimited eloquence," "power," "fearlessness" and so on, as attributes of the Buddha's state of life. To put it simply, the Buddha's concern for the people is infinite ("immeasurable mercy"), he can freely expound the teaching through words ("unlimited eloquence"), he has penetrating insight into life and the power to discern the causes of people's unhappiness ("power"), and he has the courage to fully articulate the truth ("fearlessness").

Armed with these powers of wisdom, the Buddha dives into the great ocean of the people and, while facing persecution himself, leads them to enlightenment through his wholehearted efforts.

Create a Rhythm of Continual Growth in Your Life

THE Buddha's "immeasurable mercy" includes the four infinite virtues of giving others happiness, removing their suffering, rejoicing at their happiness without any feelings of jealousy, and treating everyone impartially, abandoning attachment to prejudice and hatred. The Buddha's spirit of consideration toward the people is expansive and infinite; it knows no bounds.

In concrete terms, what does "immeasurable" mean for us as ordinary people? It means not to give up halfway. In spreading the teaching or giving individual guidance — in all aspects of the struggle for kosen-rufu — the important thing is that we follow through. Whenever we become deadlocked, we can tap inner strength through our practice to the Gohonzon and then challenge ourselves to see how many walls we can break through. Such faith to advance limitlessly may be characterized as "immeasurable."

Also, it may be hard to get a practical sense of the meaning of the spirit of compassion. President Toda used to say that "courage substitutes for compassion." Our courageous actions as emissaries of the Buddha are comparable to the Buddha's compassionate practices.

In society today, if anything, there is a tendency for people to try to avoid developing relations with others. Ours might be also characterized as a society of envy where people view the happiness of others with jealousy.

In such an environment, SGI members actively seek to develop relations with others out of the desire to help them become happy. Yet, in such a society, these compassionate actions are liable to be misunderstood and, indeed, may meet with great resistance.

Nevertheless, each day we pray and take action for others: giving people happiness, removing their sufferings, rejoicing at their happiness as if it was our own and dedicating ourselves to their well-being without discrimination. An immeasurable spirit of removing suffering and imparting joy pulses in the SGI. In this regard, we definitely stand alone.

Wherever people, instead of feeling jealous, rejoice at seeing others gain happiness, wherever people can encourage one another — that is a realm pervaded with happiness. By contrast, those who go through life constantly comparing themselves to others, consequently seesawing between joy and sorrow, find themselves utterly deadlocked in the end.

As President Toda taught, we need to live our own lives.

Just as cherry, plum, peach and damson blossoms all possess their own unique qualities, each person is unique. We cannot become someone else. The important thing is that we live true to ourselves and cause the great flower of our lives to blossom. If we fail to do so, then what is the purpose of our lives? What is the purpose of our existence?

There is no need whatsoever to compare ourselves to others. Rather, we should consider whether we have grown by comparing how we are now to how we were in the past. The Buddhist way of life is to grow each day, accomplishing more today than yesterday and more tomorrow than today.

Earnest Faith Is the Key to a Life of Freedom

NEXT, "unlimited eloquence" indicates the power to freely understand and freely express oneself without hindrance. "Unlimited eloquence" comprises four unlimited powers of understanding and preaching. These are: complete knowledge of the teachings, thorough knowledge of the meanings deriving from the teachings, complete freedom in the use of various languages and dialects to express the teachings, and the ability to preach freely and bravely, employing the other three unlimited powers.

The Buddha has the wisdom to freely understand the teachings and freely expound them. In saying that the Buddha does so "freely," we should note that while he appears to do so with composure, this is not something that happens automatically. President Toda said that even lectures on the Gosho could be classified as "unskilled," "skillful" or "artistic," pointing out that one does not all of a sudden arrive at the level of "artistic." Reaching that stage requires earnest practice and training.

The Buddha is earnest. Precisely because he is earnest, wisdom wells forth in his life. "How can I send out a message that will touch a chord in each person's life?" he continually asks. The Buddha earnestly weaves a tapestry of words. He racks his mind and exercises ingenuity. He brings to bear the power of expedient means. Such efforts find expression in his "free" preaching of the Law.

Throughout his life, Nichiren Daishonin continued to send highly detailed encouragement to his followers. Sometimes he would join them in their sadness, other times he would admonish them, show them tolerance or encourage them — all the while sending them words of revitalization. He had a thorough knowledge of the daily life, family make-up, worries and personality of each of his followers.

For example, to Sennichi-ama, after her husband, Abutsu-bo, had died, he declared that Abutsu-bo had definitely attained Buddhahood. At the same time, pointing out that her son, Tokuro Moritsuna, as a fine successor, had become a votary of the Lotus Sutra, he also says, "There is no treasure greater than a child, no treasure greater than a child!" (MW-6, 304). He thus expresses delight at the growth of a capable successor.

Another follower (Konichi-ama) was worried about her deceased son's future existence because, as a soldier, he had taken the lives of others. To this mother, the Daishonin explains the teaching that "Even a small error will destine one to the evil paths if one does not repent of it. Yet even a grave offense can be eradicated if one repents of it sincerely" (MW-4, 164). He teaches her that the child can definitely be saved from falling into the evil paths of existence through the strong faith of the parent.

Children bring their parents joy, and they also cause them worry. But the Daishonin's Buddhism teaches that, so long as they have faith, parent and child can definitely both become happy.

The Buddha's preaching is free and unrestricted. It certainly is not rigid or narrow. The Buddha knows how to explain the Law in concrete terms and based on firm principles so as to help individuals revive their spirits and create value in their situations. For this reason, the Buddha puts people's hearts at ease.

The Gosho conveys Nichiren Daishonin's words to encourage and invigorate people. One can imagine the joy of his followers upon receiving a letter from the Daishonin — right down to the look of determination that must have appeared on their faces.

The Gosho, transcending its time and place of origin, is a message of happiness for all humanity. The Gosho is a living textbook of humanism. It is the supreme inheritance of humankind.

Open a 'Path' Among the People

IN the above sutra passage, "power" refers to the ten powers of wisdom of the Buddha. For example, the Buddha has the power to judge people's understanding of the teaching, to understand their various hopes, and to know the states of life of all people.

The ten powers all revolve around the ability to understand people's minds and hearts. This ability, again, represents the crystallization of the Buddha's tenacious efforts in that regard.

The important thing is that Shakyamuni used his powers of wisdom to pioneer a path of great happiness among the people. He went out himself among the people to single-handedly spread the teaching, and he called upon his disciples to do the same. The Daishonin, too, continually expounded the Law to the people.

Unless you go out among the people, you cannot understand their hearts. For example, because Nikko Shonin spared no effort in visiting Atsuhara, the lay followers there could carry through with their faith without succumbing to the great persecution that befell them. Through Nikko Shonin's example, these followers, all of them farmers, came to understand the wondrousness of Buddhism and the Daishonin's greatness soon after they converted. And Nikko Shonin stood in the lead among them even at the height of the persecution.

Detailed reports went out from Nikko Shonin to the Daishonin, who was at Mount Minobu. Because Nikko Shonin was present on the scene, the Daishonin could gain accurate information and then take appropriate measures. It thus became possible for him to send continuous encouragement to, and open the hearts of, his followers who were in the eye of the persecution.

Because Nichiren Daishonin and Nikko Shonin had deep knowledge of the hearts of the people, they could provide the greatest encouragement, and the followers of Atsuhara could overcome the persecution.

In any age, understanding the hearts of the people is the basis for victory. A genuine leader, a true leader of Buddhism makes the greatest efforts to understand people's hearts, to understand their thoughts, and to understand their struggles.

11 — Our Concern for Kosen-rufu Enables Us To Become Buddhas

Shari-hotsu. Nyorai chiken. Kodai jinnon. Muryo muge. Riki. Mu-sho-i. Zenjo. Gedas. Sanmai. Jin nyu musai. Joju issai. Mi-zo-u ho.

"Shariputra, the wisdom of the Thus Come One is expansive and profound. He has immeasurable [mercy], unlimited [eloquence], power, fearlessness, concentration, emancipation and samadhis, and has deeply entered the boundless and awakened to the Law never before attained. (LS2, 24)

I HAVE discussed how "immeasurable mercy," "unlimited eloquence," "power" and "fearlessness" are attributes of the Buddha's life that enable him to freely expound the Law.

Of these four powers, "fearlessness" means to expound the Law bravely and without fear. It indicates the Buddha's unshakable self-confidence in expounding the Law.

The Buddha is fearless in his preaching in four ways. The first is in declaring he is enlightened to the supreme truth; that is, he has great confidence in the Mystic Law. The second is in proclaiming he has permanently extinguished all illusion; that is, he definitely will not be defeated by worries or sufferings. The third is in teaching people about delusions and hindrances that can obstruct the way to enlightenment; in other words, he encourages others to defeat the three obstacles and four devils. The fourth is in teaching people the definite path to attaining Buddhahood; that is, he vociferously proclaims he has found the path to happiness.

Fearlessness means that when talking about these things, he has no fear. In short, fearlessness means courage arising from great confidence.

If you propagate Buddhism, you are certain to meet with difficulties. Shakyamuni and Nichiren Daishonin, while fully aware of this, launched a campaign of words — their voices like the dignified roar of a lion — against the religious authorities world and the political rulers of their times. This is the epitome of fearlessness.

The Daishonin also urged his disciples to have no fear. And he said, "If Nichiren's disciples are cowardly, their prayers cannot be answered" (*GOSHO ZENSHU*, P. 840). He teaches that, while vigorously chanting the daimoku of Nam-myoho-renge-kyo, we should speak out for justice.

He indicates that such actions exemplify the spirit of this passage from the "Emerging from the Earth" chapter of the Lotus Sutra: "'[The Bodhisattvas of the Earth] are clever at difficult questions and answers, their minds know no fear'" (LS15, 223).

This passage explains that the Bodhisattvas of the Earth are skilled at discussing difficult doctrine, and that they have not the slightest fear of their opponents in debate. The Bodhisattvas of the Earth are clever at questions and answers, and they bravely stand up to even the most powerful of enemies.

If you are fearful, you cannot say anything that will strike a chord in another person's heart. Nor will any wisdom well forth in your life.

Nikko Shonin says, "You should treasure those practitioners who are skilled in difficult debate, just as the late master [Nichiren Daishonin] did" (*GOSHO ZENSHU*, P. 1619).

We should treasure boundlessly those who spread the teaching. This is Nichiren Daishonin's spirit and Nikko Shonin's decree. The priesthood today has kicked over and trampled upon this teaching, and it has persecuted the SGI — a gathering without peer or precedent of people who spread the teaching.

Highly articulate and eloquent people are treasures of kosen-rufu. Eloquence does not mean verbosity; it is the power to win others' wholehearted understanding. Sometimes even a single word from a person of strong faith is enough to win the full understanding of someone whom not even a great scholar could reach. This is the power of wisdom, the power of character, the power of faith.

Amid a storm of calumny, all of you have persistently carried out dialogue of justice, unafraid of the winds of arrogant criticism. Without doubt you qualify as people of fearlessness, as people who "are clever in difficult questions and answers."

The Buddha Freely Spreads the Law Among the People

THIS passage further explains that the Buddha possesses "concentration," "emancipation" and "*samadhis*," and that he has deeply entered a boundless state of life and become enlightened to a great Law never before attained. Because he possessed such a firm and unshakable state of life, Shakyamuni could continuously expound the Law among the people with boundless freedom.

There simply are no Buddhas who spend all their time sitting in meditation. Buddhas are Buddhas precisely because they continually ponder and take action to help others resolve their worries.

In that sense, all of you who concern yourselves over, and pray to resolve, the various problems encountered in the course of advancing kosen-rufu are most laudable. Each day, you grapple earnestly with issues relating to the happiness of friends, the advancement of kosen-rufu, and the raising of capable people. Having these concerns makes you bodhisattvas; and for the same reason, you can develop the Buddha's state of life.

Your actions to challenge the great undertaking of kosen-rufu are comparable to those of the Buddha.

As I said previously, the wisdom and powers of the Buddha indicated by this passage are attributes of the state of life embodied in the Gohonzon; and we who embrace the Gohonzon can develop this same state of life. Also, as I have already noted, "concentration," "emancipation" and "*samadhis*" are included in our practice of gongyo and chanting daimoku.

In other words, to the extent that we earnestly rack our brains for kosen-rufu, to the extent that we take our problems to the Gohonzon, these attributes of the wisdom and power of the Buddha well forth in depths of our being. This is what it means to read this passage with one's life.

In concrete terms, the Buddha's enlightened state of life and wisdom "never before attained" indicate none other than great confidence in the Gohonzon.

> *Shari-hotsu. Nyorai no. Shuju fun-betsu. Gyo ses^sho ho. Gonji Nyunan. Ekka Shushin. Shari-hotsu. Shu yo gon shi. Muryo muhen. Mi-zo-u-ho. Bus^shitsu joju.*
>
> "Shariputra, the Thus Come One knows how to make various kinds of distinctions and to expound the teachings skillfully. His words are soft and gentle and can delight the hearts of the assembly.
>
> "Shariputra, to sum it up: the Buddha has fully realized the Law that is limitless, boundless, never attained before. (LS2, 24)

IN this passage, Shakyamuni continues to praise the vast Buddha wisdom. Here, he says that, ultimately, it is because he, the Thus Come One, possesses "the Law that is limitless, boundless, never attained before," that he could skillfully expound his teachings in accordance with the people's understanding and circumstances and delight them with "soft and gentle" words.

Shakyamuni also says he could expound the Law in accordance with the worries and concerns of all people because of the abundant and profound "wisdom of the Buddhas" infusing his life. In this way, he indicates the vastness of the unparalleled Law he has attained.

This is the third time in "Expedient Means" that Shakyamuni has referred to a Law never before known or attained. Why has he said essentially the same thing to Shariputra three times since the start of the chapter?

For the voice-hearers and *pratyekabuddhas*, the "wisdom of the Buddhas" is an "infinitely profound and immeasurable" teaching that they cannot comprehend. Shakyamuni desperately wants to communicate to Shariputra and the others that there exists a realm of wisdom so vast as to be beyond even their imagination.

That is why he repeatedly alludes to the existence of a great Law never before known or attained. Shariputra and the others cannot comprehend the vast wisdom of the Buddha as long as they remain satisfied with their own shallow wisdom. For that reason, Shakyamuni courteously and repeatedly explains just how wondrous is the wisdom of the Buddhas.

One who says, "Since I explained it once, that's sufficient," lacks compassion. We should continue to conduct dialogue until the other person's life changes. Attaining the objective is what counts; to speak solely for purposes of self-satisfaction is pointless.

As he spoke each word, Shakyamuni must have been observing the changes in Shariputra's expression. While repeatedly praising the wisdom of the Buddhas, he was doubtless waiting for a great seeking spirit to arise in Shariputra's heart.

Shariputra certainly knew of Shakyamuni's greatness before this juncture. Still, his sense of respect for the grand scale of the Buddha's wisdom and his seeking spirit must have grown as he listened to Shakyamuni expound the "Expedient Means" chapter. "I wish I could hear this 'Law never before known,'" Shariputra probably thought as he aroused in himself a "seeking mind never before attained."

Praying for the Happiness of Others

"**H**IS words are soft and gentle" means that to his listeners, the Buddha's words are soft and gentle. These are words that, while tender, reverberate with piercing conviction.

With such words, the Buddha caused people to feel joy, and so led them along to this point. Even though he is saying this with regard to the [pre-Lotus Sutra] teachings he expounded "according to others' minds," it offers us an important guideline.

Here, "soft and gentle" does not simply mean kind. Such words are completely different from obsequious words intended merely to be agreeable. They are words that touch a chord in others' lives, words that move people. That is, they express an understanding of others' feelings.

Moreover, since deep down everyone desires true happiness, words uttered with ardent prayer for someone's happiness, even if they are strong, are "soft and gentle."

The Daishonin says:

> Even though one may resort to harsh words, if such words help the person to whom they are addressed, then they are worthy to be regarded as truthful words and gentle words. Similarly, though one may use gentle words, if they harm the person to whom they are addressed, they are in fact deceptive words, harsh words.

> The Buddhist doctrines preached by scholars these days are regarded by most people as gentle words, truthful words,

but in fact they are all harsh words and deceptive words. I say this because they are at variance with the Lotus Sutra, which embodies the Buddha's true intention. (MW-4, 82)

Even words that on the surface seem polite may be vicious and destroy a person's heart. By contrast, strongly spoken words can warm the heart.

There is a saying: good advice jars the ear, good medicine tastes bitter. Obsequious words are dangerous.

Conducting Hope-filled Dialogue in a Society Lacking 'Truthful Words'

WHAT are genuine "soft and gentle words"? This is not determined by how harsh or kind the words sound. Rather, it depends on whether they are laden with value, and whether there is compassion in the heart of their speaker.

In society today, "truthful words" are few. We are deluged by words of self-interest and calculation, words intended to cause injury, and words of playful caprice. These days we simply don't hear words of truth that issue from the depths of one person's heart and penetrate the heart of another.

True words coincide perfectly with the actions of the speaker. Words spoken out of personal conviction, words on the basis of which we have lived our lives are certainly true words. True words are living words that issue from a lively and exuberant heart.

Nikko Shonin admonished against indulging in "idleness and chatter" (GOSHO ZENSHU, P. 1617). Similarly, President Toda likened words not based on faith to smoke.

In conclusion, "soft and gentle words" means words spoken in good faith. Such words are sincere; they are earnest; and they have propriety. Moreover, words that clearly convey what you want to say are "soft and gentle."

A poet writes, "Abrasive words point to their weak foundation." Courteous words are a sign of self-confidence.

With abundant self-confidence, let us conduct dignified dialogue, never losing our inner latitude, poise and humor. Such dialogue is the true "weapon" of a Buddhist.

Confusion of language portends confusion in society. In an age lacking "truthful words," our movement, which is based on dialogue, is becoming a great light of hope for the world.

12 — A True Leader Brings People Joy

Shari-hotsu. Nyorai no. Shuju fun-betsu. Gyo ses^sho ho. Gonji Nyunan. Ekka Shushin. Shari-hotsu. Shu yo gon shi. Muryo muhen. Mi-zo-u-ho. Bus^shitsu joju.

"Shariputra, the Thus Come One knows how to make various kinds of distinctions and to expound the teachings skillfully. His words are soft and gentle and can delight the hearts of the assembly.

"Shariputra, to sum it up: the Buddha has fully realized the Law that is limitless, boundless, never attained before. (LS2, 24)

A LEADER is one who causes people to feel joy. The mission of a leader is to encourage people and elevate their spirits. A leader absolutely must not scold others. Nothing qualifies a leader to castigate a friend.

"Delight the hearts of the assembly" indicates that Shakyamuni delights people and wins their heartfelt understanding by means of "soft and gentle" words.

Based on firm conviction and with true "soft and gentle" words, a leader shows appreciation to everyone for their efforts, makes them feel refreshed, puts their hearts at ease, dispels their doubts and arouses their hopes and aspirations. This is a leader's struggle. Those who pressure others or drive them into a corner are disqualified as leaders and are turning their backs on this passage.

In terms of its literal meaning, this passage of "Expedient Means" describes Shakyamuni's preaching of the pre-Lotus Sutra teachings. In other words, it refers to how Shakyamuni expounded various teachings for people of different capacities and with different worries and sufferings in order to cause them to feel delight and guide them to happiness.

For example, those preoccupied with others' opinions of them, and who had lost sight of themselves, he taught to "advance on your own like the horn of a rhinoceros." On the other hand, he taught those caught up in their own narrow way of thinking that "even fools will become wise if they associate with and become close to good friends."

Also, Shakyamuni encouraged those suffering on account of desire and greed to extinguish desires, and he directed those leading hedonistic existences toward ascetic practices. On the other hand, he admonished those carrying out extended fasting or other extreme austerities to cease such painful practices and instead pursue the Middle Way.

On the surface, these different teachings might seem contradictory. But in every case, he taught people in accordance with their situations how they could improve their lives; while "delighting their hearts," he helped them advance. Shakyamuni's spirit in every instance was the same. The pre-Lotus Sutra teachings consist of the many teachings he expounded in this manner.

On the foundation of these earlier teachings, in the Lotus Sutra — irrespective of whether his listeners could readily understand — he expounds the Mystic Law, the teaching that enables people fundamentally to become happy.

Because the Buddha expounded the Lotus Sutra "according with his own mind," those hearing it could not readily comprehend it. In fact, Shariputra was so incredulous when he first heard the "Expedient Means" teaching that all people can become Buddhas that he thought, "Is this not a devil pretending to be the Buddha, trying to vex and confuse my mind?" (LS3, 50).

We cannot laugh at Shariputra. Hardly anyone, upon first hearing of Nam-myoho-renge-kyo, understands the greatness of this Buddhism or feels genuine delight. In time, however, all people can gain unsurpassed joy through this teaching. They can attain the "greatest of all joys." In that sense, the Mystic Law is the teaching that can truly "delight the hearts of the assembly." From the standpoint of Nichiren Daishonin's Buddhism, this passage means that through the benefit of the Gohonzon our lives become filled with joy.

Even though we have faith, we cannot avoid painful, sad or unpleasant things in course of life. Yet, through the principle "earthly desires are enlightenment," we can definitely manifest a state of "delight" in our lives; this is the greatness of Nichiren Daishonin's Buddhism. By advancing based on faith, we can definitely change a life of suffering into a life of great joy.

Regarding "delight the hearts of the assembly," Josei Toda, the second Soka Gakkai president, said:

> When we practice faith in earnest for ten years, our lives become truly pure. Our skin, the look of our eyes, our actions all become soft and pure, and yet come to possess a certain dignity. This is the benefit of the Gohonzon. When this happens we feel delight in our hearts; this is the meaning of "delight the hearts of the assembly."
>
> Since those who attain this state of life are always bright, they cannot help but feel joy. Such people are happy and, therefore, always smiling and cheerful; if they should go into business, they are sure to prosper. That's because others think, "If I'm going to buy the same item anyway, then I might as well go and buy it from that person." This is what "delight the hearts of the assembly" means.

Pure joy wells forth abundantly from lives polished by daimoku. People like those Mr. Toda describes are experts at life who make friends even with suffering. While skillfully keeping company with life's hardships, they can find cause for delight in any situation whatsoever. They enjoy a truly elevated state of life.

Nichiren Daishonin says, "Regard both suffering and joy as facts of life and continue chanting Nam-myoho-renge-kyo" (MW-1, 161). The central meaning is that we should regard suffering and joy as inescapable facts of our existence.

Without hardships, life would be bland and colorless. People learn from hard work; hard work provides nutrients needed to cause the flower of joy to blossom. Suffering and joy are like two sides of a coin. When we recognize this truth, we manifest the true strength of the human being and the true profundity of life.

The great Russian author Leo Tolstoy continually fought against suffering. Even when excommunicated by ecclesiastical authorities, he contemplated events with composure and poise. He retained his blazing single-minded spirit of struggle. He concluded that he would retain his creed of "rejoicing no matter what":

> Rejoice! Rejoice! One's life's work, one's mission is a joy. Toward the sky, toward the sun, toward the stars, toward the grasses, toward the trees, toward animals, toward human beings — you may as well rejoice."[1]

We train ourselves through faith to develop the state of life in which we can change everything into joy.

---

1. Translated from the Japanese: Leo Tolstoy, *Torusutoi no kotoba* (Words of Tolstoy), trans. Fumihiko Konuma, (Tokyo: Yoyoi Shobo, 1970), p. 94.

The Strong Create Value Even from Obstacles

THE Daishonin says: "The greater the hardships befalling him [the votary of the Lotus Sutra in the Latter Day of the Law], the greater the delight he feels, because of his strong faith" (MW-1, 9); and "The three obstacles and four devils will invariably appear, and the wise will rejoice while the foolish will retreat" (MW-2 [2ND ED.], 244).

Making up our minds that the greater our worries, the greater our opportunities to develop our state of life, we should advance with increasing joy and high spirits. While giving friends peace of mind, let us endure all with bright smiles on our faces and continue struggling. This is the conduct of Buddhists. Such people lead lives that "delight the hearts of the assembly." Let us live robustly.

There is a saying that "while a block of marble is an obstacle to the weak, it becomes a steppingstone to the strong."

Strong people make the most of obstacles. The stronger we are, the more joyful our lives. It all comes down to life force, spiritual energy. And these fundamentally derive from the powers of faith and practice.

Commenting on the parable of the gem in the robe from the standpoint of his Buddhism, Nichiren Daishonin explains that the joy of the poor man when he discovers that he possesses the priceless gem is "the great joy we experience when we understand for the first time that our lives have from the beginning been the Buddha. Nam-myoho-renge-kyo is the greatest of all joys" (*GOSHO ZENSHU*, P. 788).

True happiness is inner happiness. We need to establish an inner state of life that is not swayed by external conditions.

People these days tend to pursue momentary pleasures and to regard outward display of wealth as equivalent to happiness. Therefore, it is all the more important that we teach others the wonder of life's inner happiness by manifesting in our lives "the greatest of all joys."

Joy is contagious. Those who "delight the hearts of the assembly" can change those around them into people who also "delight the hearts of the assembly." And those who make efforts to "delight the hearts of the assembly" experience delight in their own hearts.

The SGI has the true capacity to "delight the hearts of the assembly." It has the joy of life and the joy of action; and because its activities are fundamentally joyful, people gather. That the SGI is joyful is great proof that Buddhism pulses vigorously in the SGI.

Become Preeminent by Practicing the Preeminent Teaching

Shi shari-hotsu. Fu shu bu setsu. Sho-i sha ga. Bus^sho joju. Dai ichi ke-u. Nange shi ho.

"But stop, Shariputra, I will say no more. Why? Because what the Buddha has achieved is the rarest and most difficult-to-understand Law. (LS2, 24)

AS I have already said, the "Expedient Means" chapter is termed the "unsolicited and spontaneous teaching." This is because the Buddha began expounding on his own initiative, saying, "The wisdom of the Buddhas is infinitely profound and immeasurable" (LS2, 23), and not in response to a question from someone else.

Up to this point, he has emphasized that the Buddha's wisdom is beyond the ability of Shariputra and others of the two vehicles to comprehend. Here, however, in order to arouse a still stronger seeking mind, Shakyamuni tells Shariputra, "I will say no more."

Live True to Yourself

SHAKYAMUNI explains that he will preach no more, "Because what the Buddha has achieved is the rarest and most difficult-to-understand Law."

President Toda, smiling, commented on this passage as follows:

> The Buddha began preaching the "Expedient Means" chapter without any question having first been put to him. Until this point, he has praised the Buddha's state of life up and down; but now he says, "I'm not going to let you hear any more." His listeners were no doubt taken aback.

Out of the desire to enable his beloved disciples to attain the supreme state of life, Shakyamuni utters the words of strict compassion, "But stop, Shariputra."

As I have noted already, the mentor's wish is to enable the disciples to attain the same state of life as he or she has. That is the true way of the mentor. A true mentor does not go out of his or her way to confuse and obstruct the growth of disciples.

Shariputra, regarded as the foremost in wisdom among Shakyamuni's disciples, listens to the preaching that follows and comes to realize that the sole purpose of Buddhist practice is to open up the world of Buddhahood in one's own life. Because he received the strictness of the mentor, Shakyamuni, with his whole being, Shariputra, the disciple, could develop his state of life.

Further, from Shakyamuni's standpoint, it was because he trusted Shariputra and his other disciples that he ventured to begin preaching the true Law, the teaching that is difficult to comprehend. If the mentor believed his disciples could not grasp his true intention, he would not have begun expounding it. With such feeble disciples, he could not even have scolded their immature state of life. Under those circumstances, he would have no choice but to expound teachings "according with others' minds" that matched his disciples' state of life.

On one level, the Lotus Sutra, and this scene in particular, might be thought of as a spiritual drama that unfolds between the mentor who begins to expound the truth and the disciples who receive his teaching with their entire beings.

From the standpoint of the Daishonin's Buddhism, this passage indicates that the great law of Nam-myoho-renge-kyo Nichiren Daishonin possesses is the "rarest" teaching, and that it is beyond people's ability to comprehend with their ordinary state of life.

The vast and boundless power of the Gohonzon cannot be fathomed with a shallow state of life. It is foolish to try to estimate or determine the power of the Gohonzon with our minds. Such thinking betrays conceit. When we practice, summoning forth great power of faith, we can definitely produce results in the form of inconspicuous and conspicuous benefit. To the extent we are convinced of this, we can expand our inner state of life.

The Mystic Law is the "rarest and most difficult-to-understand Law."

Nichiren Daishonin says, "If the Law that one embraces is supreme, then the person who embraces it must accordingly be foremost among all others" (MW-5, 32). The lives of those who embrace the supreme Law are supremely happy.

I want all of you to shine as the foremost people on your respective stages of activity. Please lead lives of brilliant proof of the supreme Law. This is what it means to practice the "rarest and most difficult-to-understand Law."

The SGI is a gathering of such foremost people. We should not demean ourselves, saying such things as, "My capability is so limited." Everyone has a mission that only he or she can fulfill.

President Toda said: "I want the rear guard of the Soka Gakkai to be a rear guard that does things beyond the ability of members of other societies. I would like to develop an organization such that even the weakest person in the Soka Gakkai is the strongest on the outside."

Determining to shine as foremost people in our respective fields of activity and to live in a manner true to ourselves, let us fulfill our missions with dignity.

13 – The True Entity of All Phenomena Is the Wisdom To Grasp the Truth of Life

WE now come to the most important passage of the "Expedient Means" chapter, the section dealing with the true entity of all phenomena and the ten factors.

Just what exactly is the wisdom of the Buddha that Shakyamuni has been praising from the start of the chapter as "infinitely profound" and "difficult to understand"? Here, he tries to explain.

The true entity of all phenomena is the wisdom of the Buddhas that can only be understood and shared between Buddhas. Shakyamuni clarifies that the true entity specifically consists of the ten factors — appearance, nature, entity, power, influence, internal cause, relation, latent effect, manifest effect, and their consistency from beginning to end.

"All phenomena" indicates life in the ten worlds (*shoho*) and its environment (*eho*), or all living beings and the realms in which they dwell. In other words, it refers to all nature, to all things and phenomena.

Also, "true entity," just as it sounds, means the true reality just as it is. The true entity of all phenomena might be thought of as the undisguised truth of all things.

134 • *Daisaku Ikeda*

The ten factors that follow indicate the contents of the true entity. For this reason, this passage is termed the "true entity of the ten factors."

Yui butsu yo butsu. Nai no kujin. Shoho jisso. Sho-i shoho. Nyo ze so. Nyo ze sho. Nyo ze tai. Nyo ze riki. Nyo ze sa. Nyo ze in. Nyo ze en. Nyo ze ka. Nyo ze ho. Nyo ze honmak^kukyo to.

The true entity of all phenomena can only be understood and shared between Buddhas. This reality consists of the appearance, nature, entity, power, influence, internal cause, relation, latent effect, manifest effect and their consistency from beginning to end." (LS2, 24)

What Are the Ten Factors?

THE meaning of the ten factors might be summarized as follows:

(1) appearance (*nyo ze so*): the external manifestation of life. (2) nature (*nyo ze sho*): the spiritual or mental aspect of life. (3) entity (*nyo ze tai*): the totality of life consisting of appearance and nature. (4) power (*nyo ze riki*): inherent energy. (5) influence (*nyo ze sa*): externally directed action. (6) internal cause (*nyo ze in*): the direct cause for

things to occur. (7) relation (*nyo ze en*): the causes or conditions that activate the internal cause. (8) latent effect (*nyo ze ka*): the result produced [in the depths of life] by internal cause and relation. (9) manifest effect (*nyo ze ho*): the concrete, perceptible manifestation of the latent effect. (10) consistency from beginning to end (*nyo ze honmatsu kukyoto*): the perfect integration of these nine factors in every moment of life.

The three factors of appearance, nature and entity explain the essential composition of all phenomena. The six factors of power, influence, internal cause, relation, latent effect and manifest effect analyze the functions and workings of all phenomena. And consistency from beginning to end indicates the coherency of the nine factors from appearance to manifest effect.

In the passage, each factor is prefixed by the term *nyo ze* (literally, "it is like"). Shakyamuni is saying in effect: although the Buddha wisdom fundamentally cannot be articulated in words, if one were to venture to describe it, this is how it might be expressed.

Let me try to explain the ten factors through an example. Your own existence is a "phenomenon." Your features, posture and so on comprise the "appearance" of the "phenomenon" of your life.

Again, while invisible to the eye, such traits as shortness of temper, magnanimity, kindness or reticence, or the various aspects of your personality or temperament, make up your "nature." Your physical and spiritual totality — that is, your "appearance" and "nature" together — make up your "entity," the person you are.

Also, your life has various energies ("power"), and these produce various external functions ("influence"). Your life thus becomes a cause ("internal cause") and, activated by conditions internal and external ("relation"), changes arise in your life ("latent effect"), and these eventually appear externally ("manifest effect").

Moreover, these nine factors interweave your life and your environment without any inconsistency or omission ("consistency from beginning to end"). This is the true aspect of the ten factors of your life.

Each of us lives within the framework of the ten factors. No one could say that he or she has no "appearance." Such a person would be invisible. Similarly, no one could truly claim not to have a personality, not to have any energy, or not to carry out any activity. Nor could there be a situation where the appearance was one person, the nature someone else and the entity another person still. There is consistency among all factors, and together they make up the irreplaceable totality of your being.

People in each of the ten worlds are endowed with the ten factors according to their state of life. For example, people in the world of Hell have the dark and depressed appearance of those overwhelmed by suffering. Since their nature is filled with suffering and anger, their power and influence tend to mire those around them in darkness, too.

Those in the world of Heaven are typically bright and smiling in their appearance. In their nature, since they feel uplifted — as though "ascending into the sky," as it were — anything they see makes them happy. Their power and influence tend to make those around them feel buoyant and cheerful, too.

Similarly, each of the ten worlds has its own factors of appearance, nature, entity, power, influence, internal cause, relation, latent effect and manifest effect, and there is consistency from beginning to end. This is the true nature of all phenomena.

President Toda explained this as follows: "Suppose there is a thief in front of us. He is a thief from appearance to manifest effect. That's consistency from beginning to end in a thief's life. There is no discontinuity."

Rather than simply looking at surface appearances, understanding the true entity of all phenomena means to grasp the vastness and profundity of life in its entirety.

The ten factors are not limited only to human beings. Flowers blooming on the roadside, for example, have the appearance, nature and entity of beauty. And they also possess power, influence, internal cause, relation, latent effect and manifest effect, without any omission. And in their totality, all of these factors are coherently integrated with the life of the flower.

The same is also true of inorganic things. A pebble, the sky, the moon, stars, the sun, the sea with its salty scent, rugged mountains, skyscrapers overlooking noisy streets, houses and cars and every piece of furniture or utensil — the ten factors describe the existence of all things.

This is the wisdom of the true entity of all phenomena that the Buddha has attained. In other words, when observing any phenomenon, the Buddha understands its true entity. When looking at people, the Buddha understands their state of life and sees their Buddha nature within. When looking at something in nature, the Buddha can sense its noble brilliance. And, considering social phenomena, the Buddha can deftly discern their underlying significance.

It might be said that the wisdom of the true entity of all phenomena is the ability to discern the true nature of all things.

The Importance of Seeing the Truth

BUDDHISM explains that there are five types of vision people may possess depending on their state of life: the eye of common mortals, the divine eye, the eye of wisdom (of people of the two vehicles), the eye of the Law (of bodhisattvas), and the eye of the Buddha. The wisdom of the true entity of all phenomena is to view everything with the eye of the Law and the eye of the Buddha.

Seeing is of course an example, but there is also hearing, smelling, tasting, feeling and sensing. Through all our faculties we should strive to perceive the true entity of all phenomena.

The French poet Comte de Lautréamont writes: "amid passing phenomena, I search for the truth."

What is important is the vision to profoundly and deftly perceive the true nature of shifting phenomena. The Buddha is one who has mastered this vision.

Often people experience failure or loss in even simple, everyday affairs due to misunderstandings or misperceptions, prejudice or speculation. It is all the more difficult to see the truth when it comes to fundamental problems of human life or society. When observing the same phenomena, the Buddha succeeds in seeing the true entity while others fail.

To take one example, the scientist Isaac Newton is said to have discovered the law of universal gravitation from observing an apple fall from a tree. In the falling apple (the phenomenon), he discerned the truth (the true entity) that the force of gravity acts upon all things. This could be thought of as a part of the wisdom of the true entity of all phenomena.

No matter how many apples someone sees fall, if the person lacks insight, he or she will not be able to discern the true entity. Newton's discovery resulted in the opening of a new world and has greatly benefited humankind.

Similarly, and on an even grander scale, the Buddha wisdom to discern the true entity of all phenomena is inestimably important for people's happiness in life, for the advancement of humanity.

To speak of discovering the true entity "behind" phenomena might give the impression that the Law exists somewhere apart from the phenomena. This is definitely not the case. Phenomena and their true entity are always inseparable. The Buddha observes the true entity as it manifests through phenomena and correctly perceives that the true entity exists only as the phenomena. They certainly do not exist separately.

To illustrate, if phenomena, which are constantly changing, are likened to waves, then the true entity is comparable to the ocean. Waves are produced by the ocean, and wave crests consist of sea water. Conversely, there is no ocean that does not manifest as waves. The two are one in essence.

Again, if the true entity is likened to the surface of a mirror, then phenomena would be comparable to the images appearing therein. The mirror reproduces all things as images. There is no mirror that does not reflect images as long as there is light. Conversely, there can be no reflected images without the mirror.

From the standpoint of life, "all phenomena" means individual lives, and "true entity" refers to the truth of life —

which pervades the universe — that the Buddha perceives. The Buddha perceives the universal life in even the smallest living manifestation.

To put it another way, all living beings are entities of the Mystic Law to which the Buddha is enlightened, and the Buddha perceives that they are inherently endowed with the Buddha nature. This is the wisdom of the true entity of all phenomena.

The vision that enables the Buddha to perceive the true entity that manifests in all phenomena is also the eye of compassion to save all people and enable them to become Buddhas.

The Daishonin says: "Life itself is the most precious of all treasures. Even the treasures of the entire universe cannot equal the value of a single human life" (MW-1, 267). The life of one person, an individual, he says, is more precious even than all the treasures of the universe. This is the wonderful Buddhist view of life, which is based on the perception of the true entity in all phenomena.

Life is mysterious. It is the wisdom of the Buddha to perfectly and fully understand the truth of life. What a vast and infinitely profound wisdom this is!

As seen with the eye of the Buddha, this world, this universe is shining with life, resounding with the chorus of all things. The Buddha perceives the irreplaceable uniqueness and value of all things in the world. The Buddha's wisdom is a state of life filled with boundless exhilaration and joy in living.

As I will discuss later, from the standpoint of the Daishonin's Buddhism, the true entity of all phenomena means the Gohonzon. For us who embrace the Gohonzon, the wisdom of the true entity of all phenomena means to view everything with the eye of Buddhism and the eye of faith.

14 – The Gohonzon Is the True Entity of All Phenomena

Yui butsu yo butsu. Nai no kujin. Shoho jisso. Sho-i shoho. Nyo ze so. Nyo ze sho. Nyo ze tai. Nyo ze riki. Nyo ze sa. Nyo ze in. Nyo ze en. Nyo ze ka. Nyo ze ho. Nyo ze honmak^kukyo to.

The true entity of all phenomena can only be understood and shared between Buddhas. This reality consists of the appearance, nature, entity, power, influence, internal cause, relation, latent effect, manifest effect and their consistency from beginning to end." (LS2, 24)

IN my last lecture, I discussed the wisdom of the Buddha who has realized the true entity existing in all things from the standpoint of the sutra passage revealing the ten factors of life.

In "The True Entity of Life," Nichiren Daishonin clarifies the fundamental meaning of the true entity of the ten factors.

The Daishonin wrote "The True Entity of Life" in reply to a question from his disciple Sairen-bo regarding the above passage of the "Expedient Means" chapter. Sairen-bo, who is thought to have been originally a scholar-priest of the Tendai school, was an avid student of Buddhism.

The Daishonin plainly states at the outset of this Gosho that the Lotus Sutra passage explaining the ten factors of life "means that all beings and their environments in any of the ten worlds, from Hell at the lowest to Buddhahood at the highest, are, without exception, the manifestations of Myoho-renge-kyo" (MW-1, 89). In other words, all life (all phenomena), which undergoes constant and manifold changes, is the manifestation of Nam-myoho-renge-kyo (the true entity).

The entire universe is itself the Mystic Law. All things in nature are the song, the dance, the drama, the poem, the sparkling, the birth and death, the suffering and joy, the constant vicissitudes, the advance and the supreme joy of the Mystic Law.

We practice faith to become genuinely aware of the true entity of all phenomena and to manifest it actively in our own lives. Through faith, we can develop a great state of absolute freedom in our lives.

Of the ten factors of life, "consistency from beginning to end" does not mean simply that the nine factors from "appearance" to

Lectures on the "Expedient Means" Chapter • 143

"manifest effect" are perfectly integrated in each of the ten worlds — so that if someone or something is in the world of Hell, for instance, then all factors of that person or thing will be in the state of Hell. The Daishonin clarifies that it indicates consistency on a more fundamental level, that all nine factors in any of the ten worlds are fundamentally manifestations of Myoho-renge-kyo.

To view all things as manifestations of Myoho-renge-kyo is to perceive the true entity of all phenomena. This is the wisdom of the Buddha.

In another Gosho, the Daishonin clearly says, "The ten factors of life are Myoho-renge-kyo" (*GOSHO ZENSHU*, P. 415). Nam-myoho-renge-kyo is the fundamental law of the universe (the true entity) that ceaselessly manifests as life in the ten worlds (all phenomena).

One who becomes enlightened to the Mystic Law as the fundamental truth of the universe is the Buddha. The Buddha's enlightened state of life is expressed as the Gohonzon. Therefore, the ten factors of life ultimately indicate the Gohonzon.

President Toda explained this, saying:

> The ten factors thus become an abbreviated explanation of the form of the Gohonzon. That's why the "Expedient Means" chapter is very important.
>
> On the surface, they are just the ten factors; this is on the level of doctrinal study of sutras. But from the standpoint of the enlightenment of Nichiren Daishonin, on the level of his perception of the truth in the depths of his being, they become a description of the Gohonzon.

In other words, from the standpoint of the Daishonin's Buddhism, the true entity of all phenomena is none other than the Gohonzon.

In terms of the Gohonzon, "Nam-myoho-renge-kyo Nichiren" inscribed down the center of the Gohonzon corresponds to the true entity, and the beings of the ten worlds appearing on either side represent all phenomena. In terms of the doctrine of *ichinen sanzen*, *ichinen* (a single life-moment) corresponds to the true entity, and *sanzen* (three thousand realms) to all phenomena.

When we pray to the Gohonzon of actual *ichinen sanzen*, as beings of the nine worlds, our daily activities, illuminated by Nam-myoho-renge-kyo, reveal the true entity of all phenomena. The Daishonin says, "The living beings of the ten worlds are all Buddhas of the true entity of all phenomena" (*GOSHO ZENSHU*, P. 830). Our lives just as they are — whether in the world of Hell or the world of Humanity — can shine as the embodiment of the true entity, that is, of Myoho-renge-kyo.

It is not necessary to go far away or to become someone special. Regardless of whether we experience suffering or joy, as long as we sincerely continue to pray to the Gohonzon and take action for kosen-rufu, then, just as we are, we will definitely become Buddhas of the true entity of all phenomena. And we can fulfill our own unique mission.

In fact, through our practice of faith we become able to express the unimpeded workings of *ichinen sanzen* in our day-to-day existence and throughout our lives.

The twenty-sixth high priest, Nichikan, says in his exegesis on "The True Object of Worship": "When we single-mindedly chant Nam-myoho-renge-kyo, our lives in their entirety become the object of worship."

Through carrying out the practice of the Mystic Law for ourselves and others, our lives become the Gohonzon. We can in fact make our lives shine as entities of the Mystic Law.

President Toda said: "By worshiping the Gohonzon and chanting Nam-myoho-renge-kyo, the Gohonzon thoroughly penetrates our lives. When we open our eyes and look at the universe, there we find the Gohonzon. And when we close our eyes and look deeply within, the Gohonzon clearly appears there, too, all the while increasing in strength and coming to shine still more brightly."

Fundamentally, the entire universe is the true entity of all phenomena and the Gohonzon. Fundamentally, our own lives are also the true entity of all phenomena and the Gohonzon. Therefore, when we worship the Gohonzon, through the dynamic exchange between the universe and our lives, our own true entity — that is, our lives as the entity of Nam-myoho-renge-kyo — comes to shine. The wisdom of the Buddha inherent in our lives wells forth. The courage to take compassionate action arises in our hearts. And we enter the golden path of happiness.

How great, indeed, is the Gohonzon! How wondrous is the wisdom of the Lotus Sutra! Let us deeply engrave in our hearts that the Gohonzon itself is the embodiment of inexhaustible happiness and wisdom, and it is the Lotus Sutra of the Latter Day of the Law.

The Mutual Possession of the Ten Worlds and *Ichinen Sanzen*

THROUGH explaining the ten factors and the true entity of all phenomena, Shakyamuni has more or less expressed the contents of the wisdom of the Buddha. Later on in the "Expedient Means" chapter, he explains the Buddha's one teaching (the one Buddha vehicle) that "opens the door of," "shows," "awakens living beings to," and "induces them to enter" the path of the Buddha wisdom. And he clarifies that the three types of teachings (the three vehicles) expounded before the Lotus Sutra for the voice-hearers, *pratyekabuddhas* and bodhisattvas are expedient means. This is called the "replacement of the three vehicles with the one vehicle."

Since the passage explaining the true entity of the ten factors indicates the gist of the replacement, it is termed the concise replacement of the three vehicles with the one vehicle. The Great Teacher T'ien-t'ai of China established his essential doctrine of *ichinen sanzen* on the basis of this passage and the concept of the mutual possession of the ten worlds.

The teaching of the Lotus Sutra that opens the wisdom of the Buddha to all people is the revelation that all beings of the nine worlds are endowed with the world of Buddhahood. Based on this mystic principle, T'ien-t'ai expressed the inscrutable true entity through the concepts of the mutual possession of the ten worlds (that each of the ten worlds is endowed with all ten worlds) and the hundred worlds and thousand factors (that each of the hundred worlds is endowed with the ten factors).

The realm of the environment is then clarified when we come to the indication, in the "Life Span of the Thus Come One" chapter of the essential teaching of the Lotus Sutra, that this *saha* world is the land where the Buddha dwells eternally. On this basis, T'ien-t'ai develops the doctrine of *ichinen sanzen*, explaining that the thousand factors contain the three realms.

In this connection, Nichiren Daishonin says, "The doctrine of *ichinen sanzen* arises from the ten factors contained in the first volume [of the eight volumes] of the Lotus Sutra" (*GOSHO ZENSHU*, P. 412).

And so we see that the passage explaining the true entity of the ten factors is a crucial one indicating that the beings of the ten worlds can all become Buddhas.

To say that the beings of the ten worlds all possess the ten factors — appearance, nature, entity, power, influence, inherent cause, relation, latent effect, manifest effect and their consistency from beginning to end — is nothing less than an affirmation that, as seen with the eye of the Buddha, there is no difference between the life of the Buddha and the lives of others. The enlightenment of all people, therefore, is a certainty.

The Daishonin emphasizes the importance of this passage, saying:

> The ultimate purpose of the Buddha's advent in this world is the Lotus Sutra, the fundamental teaching that enables all living beings to enter the Buddha Way. This doctrine, however, is to be found only in the four-character phrase of the true entity of all phenomena.... This single phrase contains immense meaning. (*GOSHO ZENSHU*, P. 1139)

Refutation of the Tendai School for Their Lack of Practice

TRULY epochal significance attaches to the fact that, from the standpoint of the Daishonin's teaching, the true entity of all phenomena is the Gohonzon.

The purpose of T'ien-t'ai's Buddhism was to perceive the true entity of all phenomena in one's own heart through the practice of observing one's mind and perceiving the Law therein. The ultimate target was to awaken to the true entity at one with all phenomena.

However, this spirit was distorted by later Tendai scholars. The Tendai school in the Daishonin's day had declined even to the point of repudiating the value of Buddhist practice. Their view, simply put, was that since the true entity was at one with all phenomena, then it was fine for things to be just as they were; one was a Buddha even if he or she carried out no practice. They had become completely degenerate; they had killed the spirit of the founder, T'ien-t'ai.

Simply saying that reality, mired in pollution and suffering, is itself the true entity cannot possibly lead to improvement in people's lives or in society. To this day, the tendency to readily view present conditions with rose-colored glasses and neglect the action needed to bring about positive change remains deeply ingrained in Japanese people's outlook on religion and on life.

Nichiren Daishonin fought against this decadent Tendai school. It could even be said that priests of the Tendai school used the teaching of the true entity of all phenomena to justify their own decadence. In this respect they resemble the Nichiren Shoshu priesthood today.

Lectures on the "Expedient Means" Chapter • 149

The Daishonin revived the wisdom of the Buddha who perceived the true entity of all phenomena as a guideline for people to strive toward in their Buddhist practice and use to attain Buddhahood. That is, he inscribed the Gohonzon that embodies the enlightened life of the Thus Come One of Nam-myoho-renge-kyo (Nichiren Daishonin) for all people throughout the world during the Latter Day of the Law.

The Daishonin's Buddhism teaches not that we should merely observe the true entity of all phenomena within our lives but that we should strive to make the reality of our lives and our environment shine as the true entity of all phenomena. It is a philosophy of change and improvement for causing all phenomena — our lives and society — to shine as the entity of the Mystic Law.

With the light of the wisdom of the true entity of all phenomena, we can dispel the darkness of illusion arising from ignorance of this wisdom. In that sense, our existence itself is light. Ours is a struggle to brighten and illuminate the place where we are. When we become light, then, no matter where we are, there can be no darkness in that realm.

The Daishonin initiated a great struggle of religious reformation to refute the decadence and degeneration of the Buddhist world. And we, who have a direct connection in faith with the Daishonin, carry on this struggle.

The Nichiren Shoshu priesthood today, similar to the Tendai school in the Daishonin's time but incomparably more reprehensible, has trampled upon the founder's spirit. Neglecting practice and whiling away their lives in dissipation, they have thoroughly defiled the spirit of Buddhism. Therefore, we have struggled dauntlessly against them. Fighting evil is proof of a true disciple of the Daishonin.

The Benefit of Reading the Passage Three Times

WHAT significance attaches to our reading this passage explaining the true entity of the ten factors three times when we recite the sutra during our practice of gongyo each morning and evening?

This is based on a statement the Daishonin makes in the Gosho "The Doctrine of *Ichinen Sanzen*." He explains that reading the ten factors three times signifies the manifestation of the three truths — non-substantiality, temporary existence and the Middle Way — in our lives. This means that our lives manifest the three enlightened properties of the Law, wisdom and action. It also means that our lives manifest the three virtues of the property of the Law, wisdom and emancipation.

Our lives shine as Buddhas embodying enlightenment (the property of Law) endowed with wisdom (the property of wisdom) and compassion (the property of action and emancipation). The Daishonin teaches, "There is increased benefit in reading [this passage] three times" (*GOSHO ZENSHU*, P. 412). In short, we read it three times to proclaim that our lives are noble Buddhas and increase our benefit of faith.

In general, every time we do gongyo and chant daimoku, we praise the Buddha nature in our own lives. We also praise the Buddha nature in the lives of all others, and we commune with the Buddha nature of the universe. What a solemn ceremony this is! How fortunate we are to live according to the principle of faith manifesting itself in daily life!

15 – In Suffering or Joy, We Can Find Meaning

Yui butsu yo butsu. Nai no kujin. Shoho jisso. Sho-i shoho. Nyo ze so. Nyo ze sho. Nyo ze tai. Nyo ze riki. Nyo ze sa. Nyo ze in. Nyo ze en. Nyo ze ka. Nyo ze ho. Nyo ze honmak^kukyo to.

The true entity of all phenomena can only be understood and shared between Buddhas. This reality consists of the appearance, nature, entity, power, influence, internal cause, relation, latent effect, manifest effect and their consistency from beginning to end." (LS2, 24)

WHAT does the wisdom of the true entity of all phenomena add to our lives? It gives us the power to skillfully use everything that happens to create value.

Many things occur in the course of life. There are sufferings and joys, tailwinds and headwinds. All such phenomena provide opportunities for us to make the true entity of the world of Buddhahood in our lives shine; we can use everything that happens to expand our happiness. This is what it means to lead a life illuminated by the wisdom of the true entity of all phenomena.

Worth is not found in joy alone. Nor is success the only valuable outcome. Suffering is the mother of realization; worries and failures, so long as we are not defeated by them, enable us to deepen our faith. Our sufferings become the raw material with which to construct our happiness. This is the principle of "earthly desires are enlightenment." Earthly desires, like other phenomena, are themselves the true entity.

Fundamentally, for people with faith in the Gohonzon, everything that happens is a benefit. This is the difference between those who believe in the Mystic Law and those who do not.

As a young man, I once asked President Toda what makes a person great. Brightly smiling, he replied: "It's having confidence. In life and in everything, it's confidence that counts."

There are many important things in life. Among all possible answers, Mr. Toda, without a moment's hesitation, cited confidence. By this, he meant of course great confidence in the Mystic Law.

"I will show victory in my life without fail." "I will help everyone definitely become happy." "I will cause my workplace and my community to develop greatly." "I will change the current of the times toward the emergence of a joyous society of humanism." Those who possess and who take unwavering action based on such confidence are great.

Confidence is single-minded resolve. Confidence is courage. Confidence is hope. Confidence is inner latitude and mercy. As the twenty-sixth high priest, Nichikan, indicates when he says, "Buddhahood means a strong mind of faith in the Lotus Sutra," confidence is itself the world of Buddhahood.

Although confidence and the world of Buddhahood are invisible to the eye, they are certain to become manifest in concrete form. This is in accordance with the principle of the true entity manifesting in all phenomena. Buddhism is not empty idealism.

Faith Manifests Itself in Daily Life

BUDDHISM becomes manifest in society. It could be said that Buddhism is the "true entity," and society (secular matters) "all phenomena." Similarly, faith is the "true entity" and daily life "all phenomena." The principle of faith manifesting itself in daily life is thus the principle of the true entity of all phenomena.

There can be no Buddhism divorced from the real world. The Daishonin, citing T'ien-t'ai's words, "No affairs of life or work are in any way different from the ultimate reality," says: "A person of wisdom is not one who practices Buddhism apart from worldly affairs but, rather, one who thoroughly understands the principles by which the world may be governed" (MW-6, 142); and "secular matters ultimately are Buddhism" (MW-1, 269). "Ultimately," here means "just as they are." In other words, secular matters, just as they are, are Buddhism. Only in the real world can the validity of Buddhism be proven.

Nichiren Daishonin teaches: "When the skies are clear, the ground is illuminated. Similarly, when one knows the Lotus Sutra, he understands the meaning of all worldly affairs" (MW-1, 82). President Toda commented on this passage of "The True Object of Worship" as follows: "The Daishonin is saying that those who have embraced the Gohonzon ought to know, for example, how to improve their lives or how to develop their business."

The sun instantaneously illuminates the earth. Likewise, those who uphold the Mystic Law have to understand secular matters. Faith causes the sun of wisdom — which enables us to clearly see what we need to do in order to win — to rise in our hearts.

One of the Buddha's ten honorable titles is "Understanding of the World." The Buddha has a profound understanding of all secular affairs.

The Ten Factors Also Exist in the Land

INCIDENTALLY, the true entity of the ten factors exists in the land and in society, just as it does in our lives and in our day-to-day existences. The land and society, for instance, have the factors of inherent cause and latent effect. They also have power. The "destiny," "good fortune" or other such characteristics of a land or society manifest in its appearance.

Nichiren Daishonin writes: "Buddhism is like the body and society like the shadow. When the body is crooked, so is the shadow" (MW-3, 308). A body and its shadow are an inseparable

Lectures on the "Expedient Means" Chapter • 155

unity. If crookedness in the "body" — distortions of philosophy, thought and religion — are not rectified, then all attempts to produce a straight "shadow" are bound to fail.

Through our movement to conduct dialogue, we contribute to society on a fundamental level by helping straighten out this "body." We are creating the fundamental inherent cause for peace and prosperity.

This August marks the fiftieth anniversary of the end of World War II — a great war that plunged the entire world into hellish suffering. And yet, even now, new tragedies are unfolding in the world.

No land is more wretched than one wracked by ceaseless hostilities and bloodshed. War destroys everything. Nothing is more cruel than war.

President Toda, thinking of the suffering of the people of North and South Korea during the Korean War, composed the following elegy:

> I grieve for the many people there must be who have lost their husbands or wives, or who search in vain for their children or parents, on account of this war.

> There must be those who, losing the wealth that they have accumulated, are reduced to beggary and suddenly die.

> There are doubtless young people who have died without knowing why. And elderly women who have been killed while crying out, "I haven't done anything wrong!"

> There must be bands of children who cannot even imagine what it would be like to have parents and siblings. And there are doubtless not a few housewives who have come to regard it as normal to be living with just the clothes on their backs, and elderly people surprised to find themselves dreaming about the rice they once ate.
>
> Are there not some who show surprise when asked, "Whose side are you on?" and who reply without hesitation, "I am on the side of food and shelter."

These lines express the grief, sadness, anger and resentment of people mercilessly trampled upon, divided and killed. President Toda regarded the sufferings of the people of Asia as his own, and he was deeply pained by their plight. In his heart, he shed tears of sympathy. And, to wipe away the tears of all people, he stood up alone to undertake the great struggle to widely propagate the Mystic Law.

Carrying on the spirit of our mentor, we help friends become happy through the Mystic Law and send brilliant waves of peace, culture and education across the globe.

Creating a True and Lasting Peace

THE true entity of all phenomena is the philosophical principle of the sanctity of life.

In the world today, ethnic conflicts and fear of terrorism are intensifying. The tragedy of people hating and killing their fellow human beings goes on with no sign of abating.

Even in Japan, murders involving firearms are on the increase, and there is a growing sense of anxiety about the emergence of a "handgun society."

However, as seen with the eye of the Buddha who recognizes that each person is an entity of the Mystic Law, each person — irrespective of ethnicity, social standing or birth — is truly invaluable and irreplaceable. There must be no discrimination. The killing of people in society is absolutely intolerable.

"May all people shine! May all life shine!" This cry of love for humanity is the cry of the Lotus Sutra. It is the cry of those who understand the true entity of all phenomena. Buddhism exists to enable all people to share in the boundless joy of life.

Therefore, it is the duty of Buddhists to struggle dauntlessly against those who would rob life of its sanctity. In his famous "Declaration on the Abolition of Nuclear Weapons," President Toda proclaimed that he wanted "to root out the talons hidden behind" nuclear weapons.

It was a challenge against the devilish nature inherent in life that would prompt people to employ nuclear weapons against one another, and against the power of the *mara,* the "robber of life," pervading the universe. It was a battle against the invidious nature of authority that readily uses people and sacrifices their lives in the interest of its own self-preservation.

The dawn of the twenty-first century is just before us. Humankind must overcome on its own this devilish nature, this cancer of humanity, that has festered and grown to sickening proportions during the twentieth century.

The Lotus Sutra's wisdom of the true entity of all phenomena will undoubtedly become an important guideline for the new century — for realizing a century free of murder, a century in which people can peacefully coexist with one another and with nature.

In that sense, all of you spreading the Mystic Law are pioneers. You will definitely win the applause of the new century.

From the standpoint of the true entity of all phenomena, to harm someone is to harm the universe and to harm oneself.

When such a sense of oneness with the universe is lost, people become isolated and alienated from one another like grains of sand, and violence erupts from the depths of their impoverished, nihilistic hearts.

When a sense of oneness with the infinite life that is the Mystic Law is established in people's lives, it doubtlessly will feel as though humankind has been liberated from prison.

Nichiren Daishonin says: "Ultimately, all phenomena are contained within one's life, down to the last particle of dust. The nine mountains and the eight seas are encompassed by one's body; the sun, moon and myriad stars are contained within one's mind" (MW-5, 181).

The mountains and oceans, the sun, moon and stars, the Daishonin says, are all encompassed in one's being; what a vast and grand state of life he describes! The Gohonzon reveals the vast life of the original Buddha, who realizes the unity of the universe with the self, the self with the universe. The Daishonin, out of his immense compassion, bestowed the Gohonzon on humankind so that we, too, might develop the same state of life.

We find similar insights outside the Buddhist tradition as well. For example, the English author D.H. Lawrence (1885-1930) writes:

Lectures on the "Expedient Means" Chapter • 159

> I am part of the sun as my eye is part of me. That I am part of the earth my feet know perfectly, and my blood is part of the sea. My soul knows that I am part of the human race, my soul is an organic part of the great human soul, as my spirit is part of my nation.[1]

He is expressing a sense of the oneness of the individual life and the universe. This true aspect of human life has been pursued through various philosophies, religions and literatures of East and West since time immemorial. The Daishonin's Buddhism perfectly expresses the unity of life with the universe both theoretically and in practical terms. The Daishonin's Buddhism, therefore, might be characterized as a religion of universal humanism.

Lawrence, who looked forward to the arrival of a new age of humankind, concludes, "Start with the sun, and the rest will slowly, slowly happen."[2]

Buddhism comes down to state of life. "Start with the sun." While carrying out a dialogue with the heavens, and with the gods of the sun and moon as our allies, we are developing a magnificent state of life. This is our Buddhist practice.

What is the purpose of life? It is to construct and solidify a state of absolute happiness, a condition in which to be alive is itself great joy.

Whatever happens we experience joy. In the depths of our lives, we are always happy. And we have confidence in the

---

1. D.H. Lawrence, *Apocalypse* (New York: Penguin Books, 1976), p. 126.
2. Ibid.

future. Like the ocean that remains calm in its depths even when waves rage over its surface during storms, and like the sun that continues shining on high even during heavy rain when dark clouds fill the sky, at every turn we can create value and develop our state of life, enjoying our existence to the fullest in times of both suffering and joy. This is a life based on the true entity of all phenomena.

How wonderful, indeed, are the lives that we who dedicate ourselves to Nichiren Daishonin's "Buddhism of the sun" can lead! And what a brilliant dawn for human civilization this great Buddhism will bring on! As we approach the twenty-first century, we will see increasingly clear actual proof of this. Burning with this great confidence, let us advance toward our tomorrow.